WISE WOMEN SPEAK

CHOOSING
STEPPING
STONES
ALONG
THE
PATH

WISE
WOMEN
SPEAK

choosing

stepping

stones

along

the path

COMPILED BY

FERN CARNESS
MPH, RN

AND

LISA EDWARDS
MBA, RD

Cover: A photographic pathway depicts stepping stones planted among peaceful grounds scattered with enchanting blossoms and blooms. Sections of life's pathway have been quilted together symbolizing the coming together of 20 empowering life stories, of 20 incredible women who are walking different paths, yet perhaps the same path.

Lyrics to We Are All Angels used with permission of songwriters Michael Gott and Karen Drucker as sung by Karen Drucker and quoted in chapter written by Lisa Edwards.

Editor: Sandra Wendel
Write On, Inc., Omaha
www.health-eheadlines.com

Text design by Gary Grubbs
Freestyle Graphics, Omaha
comarts4u@aol.com
(402) 691-0950

Cover design by Lou Anne Zacek Baker
L A Design Co., Omaha
www.ladesignco.com
www.louannebaker.com
ladesco@yahoo.com
(402) 880-5195
(402) 292-2796

Printed by Banta Book Group
Eden Prairie, Minnesota

Carness Health Management, LLC
PO Box 509
Lake Oswego, OR 97034
(503) 636-7513

To order additional books or to inquire about Wise Women Speak seminars, please contact Lisa Edwards (916) 714-1683 or Fern Carness (503) 636-7513

Contents

Introduction

I am constantly amazed at what can happen when you put powerful, extraordinary women together and let the magic begin. We've done it again in this, the second book in the Wise Women Speak series.

The first book *Wise Women Speak: 20 Ways to Turn Stumbling Blocks into Stepping Stones* continues to be highly successful. The book itself has more power than the sum of the individual stories – as does this book. Nine of us authors found ourselves on stage at the National Wellness Conference in Wisconsin during the summer of 2002 to simply read our own stories to the eager audience. The energy in the room was electric. Not a dry eye from the moment Jennifer Hays said, "My first thought was this can't be true. This cannot be really happening . . ." until Elaine Sullivan closed by sharing her life's work – helping women tell their stories.

Women coming together to share stories with other women. We laughed, we cried, we danced. It doesn't get any better than this.

Now we present to you the second book in this series. Once again 20 women from 20 different walks of life come together to share their hearts and bare their souls. Each chapter begins with a story of fragility and strength and closes with a summing up of life's lessons learned.

In the first book we offered stories of women overcoming obstacles to find a stepping stone to land on. Now we present stories of how to choose the stepping stone wisely as we move along the path.

Regardless of what path you are on, you will find strength, grace, and life lessons among these pages. Along my life path, I found Lisa Edwards, a dear friend who willingly took on the task of producing this book for us. Little did she know it would be a bit like herding cats to get 20 women to do the same thing at the same time and on time.

Make a pot of tea, grab a quilt to snuggle up with, sit back, and breathe. Enjoy. I know you will.

With your health in mind,

Fern Carness

Every woman knows that life has shaped the person she is. We do not always recognize how our paths have been carefully chosen. We must let life's experience do its work and listen to our innate wisdom that will seek the path we are meant to walk.

The women I have been fortunate to come to know while gathering these stories bring amazing dimension to a wealth of experience. They have touched my life in profound ways, as I know they will touch yours. Open your mind and let their lessons be your own. There is something in this book for every woman. Thank you, Fern, for inviting me to be a part of bringing these wise women together – the authors and readers will live more fully because you had the vision.

Wishing you clarity in purpose,

Lisa Edwards

Pregnant with Fear

Stephanie Koraleski, PhD

Stephanie Koraleski, PhD, is a licensed psychologist in the Behavioral Health department at one of the largest hospital systems in Omaha, Nebraska – Methodist Health System. She is a diplomate with the American Board for Clinically Certified Hypnotherapists, a Reiki master, and a student of healing touch and EMDR (Eye Movement Desensitization and Retraining). Her current practice includes people diagnosed with cancer, chronic pain, multiple sclerosis, cardiac and pulmonary diseases, infertility, fibromyalgia, and post-traumatic stress disorder.

Stephanie worked as a career counselor and therapist in two university counseling centers, a psychiatric hospital, and an outpatient counseling center before returning to school to get her doctoral degree. Since earning her PhD in 1996 at the University of Nebraska, she has worked in the Behavioral Health area where she conducts therapy with individual patients and families, facilitates support groups, and provides training and consulting to medical staff about the psychological and emotional impact of disease on the people affected.

She has been an invited presenter at the nation's largest wellness gathering, the National Wellness Conference, for the past three years speaking on topics including mind-body wellness and living with chronic illness. This chapter is adapted from her forthcoming book, *I Just Want My Life Back: How to Find Balance When Illness Rocks Your World.*

Stephanie Koraleski, PhD
Behavioral Health
Methodist Hospital Cancer Center
8303 Dodge Street
Omaha, NE 68114
(402) 354-5893

My Story

I was 43 years old with three sons 10, 14, and 17. I was working as a mental health therapist, enrolled full time in a doctoral program, and doing a part-time internship. Life was chaotic and good. Then I developed a strangely familiar flu. It hung around for a couple of weeks, leaving me feeling tired and queasy. When my breasts began to swell, I was incredulous. I couldn't be pregnant! All three boys had been mega fertility drug babies; this couldn't happen to me. But there was the home pregnancy kit telling me a baby was growing inside.

My husband was as shocked as I was. And you haven't lived until you've told your high school senior that he's going to be a big brother – again. But within a couple of months we were getting excited and beginning to think a baby could be very fun, especially when the ultrasound tech told us this would be a little girl. So it felt like a bomb exploding in my soul when my physician called me at home and said there was a problem. He told me that a test indicated that my little baby had a neural tube defect and that this would mean her disabilities would range from spina bifida to being born without a brain. He suggested that I still had time to "do something about this." In my shock, I thought he meant vitamins or some kind of prenatal surgery. He meant abortion.

I couldn't go there. As a therapist I had worked with many women who had made that decision; no one I knew had ever made it easily, and each had suffered in the aftermath in her own way. I talked to my husband and I prayed.

I decided against further testing because I knew I couldn't live through an abortion any more than the baby could. I told my husband that I needed to just focus on the baby, not the defects. I needed to give birth, look at the child, name her, and then deal with whatever problems might be. My husband supported me. We told the physician his job was to deliver the baby safely and keep me healthy and we would decide after her birth what we would do next. We also decided not to tell our families because we didn't want them to worry. We knew we couldn't cope with anyone else's anxiety when we already had so much of our own.

The next six months were equal to my entire graduate school experience in learning about dealing with emotional problems. I was scared. I was depressed. I was in denial. I was obsessing. I was standing in the middle of Walgreen's picking up a prescription for one of the boys when I had a panic attack. It was an odd experience for me. Here I was, a middle-aged therapist, standing in Walgreen's with a racing heart, pounding head, wanting to bolt through the store screaming. And all the while the little voice in my head was saying, "Steph, this is a panic attack. Stand still, breathe, focus on something else." So I walked up and down the aisles looking at extension cords and vaporizers until I could breathe, then got my prescription and went home. It was a long six months.

When an unwanted health problem comes into your life and decides to take up residence for awhile, you may not be able to live the way you have always lived. Health problems are stressful whether they involve waiting for a baby who may have problems, awaiting a diagnosis for your symptoms, receiving treatment for cancer or rehabilitation for heart disease, or living with a chronic illness. It takes time and energy to manage your health, get to your doctors' appointments, deal with your treatment, and organize your life. Most people find that life needs reworking and some things will have to go. This is a difficult process that involves several steps.

Let me share this journey with you.

Stephanie Koraleski

Pregnant with Fear

Be realistic about your limits.

Almost any healthy young person can burn both ends of the candle for a day, a week, or even a month in a crunch. No one can live that way much longer without major mental or physical consequences.

During the stressful pregnancy, I was morning sick. I was heart-sick. I was exhausted. I realized that I couldn't work a part-time job and an internship and go to school and be a wife and mom while I was pregnant and so scared. My family roots are deep in immigrants and pioneers. I always used to say our unwritten family motto was "we do what we have to do." But this time, even though I hated to admit it, I couldn't "rise above this." It was eating me up and I couldn't give my full attention to my patients' needs as well as I was used to doing. I could barely keep my family clean and fed.

If you are in a similar situation, be honest. How much energy do you really have? What does it take to build your energy? What drains it? Energy is like a bank account. Life is much better if you live with a positive balance. I realized that this new "energy flow" problem was draining my balance faster than I could refill it. Something had to go.

Trim your life to fit inside your limits.

This is harder. Figuring out what to cut is some of the most excruciating work people need to do. It's like the old group exercise where you are told about 10 people on a life raft and then have to decide who to throw overboard because you can only save five. This is what counselors call "values clarification." It's a lot more fun in workshops than in your real life.

In my life, I had to choose among my health, my baby, my exist-ing family, my education, my job, and the patients I was committed to. I loved them all. Ultimately I decided to finish the internship, quit the job, and take less coursework. It almost killed me to quit my job. I felt so guilty leaving my patients, especially the ones who were in the middle of difficult therapy. Ultimately I had to make a "Sophie's choice." I knew I was the only one who could carry the baby inside;

I had wonderful colleagues who could support my patients. I had to choose to keep the baby on my raft, but it was a heartbreaking decision.

Get support.

When you have to do something extremely difficult for more than a week or two, you begin to feel the toll. The energy is flowing out faster than you can bring more in. You need to identify what makes you stronger and actively work to acquire that strength.

I needed some rest and some time to get past the morning sickness. I could figure that out by myself. But what I really needed was a lot of love and support. I felt like a rotten person — a quitter, a coward. I wasn't ready to talk to many friends or to worry my family members, so I found a great therapist. She listened compassionately while I talked about everything that ever bothered me — everything except what was really wrong. And that was OK for then. I wasn't ready to talk about that. But I took a lot of strength from her kindness and care. She helped me put old guilts and fears to rest. She mothered me so I could feel strong enough to face mothering this child.

Different people and different situations call for different types of support. Think about what you need and give yourself the best you can get. For some people that will mean getting a second or even third opinion from physicians. For others it may mean trying medications to help with anxiety or depression. Some folks may benefit from trying support groups or therapy groups. Other people find their best support comes from a minister, rabbi, priest, or spiritual director.

You won't know what helps until you try it, so if your anxieties aren't calming under your own efforts, try something or someone else. Don't let lack of money hold you back. There are many wonderful practitioners at clinics that base fees on the client's income. Many churches sponsor counseling clinics. Psychologists and counselors are urged in their code of ethics to donate some services without charge. University counseling students and massage therapy students have to put in hundreds of hours in low-cost school-run clinics before they can get licensed. These are often very good people who have the time and energy to focus on you. If you don't like the person or the work doesn't seem helpful, you don't have to go back. Just keep looking.

There is help available.

Admit your worst fears.

When you are faced with an extreme challenge, you have many fears. Most of them are distractions; real enough, but you know you would handle them. Underneath those are the really bad fears, the worst fears, the ones that make you wonder whether you could live if they happened. These are the ones that you need to find the courage to face.

As I work with my cancer patients now, I find that even though their diseases may be similar, their fears are quite different. Some people are afraid of being in terrible pain. Others are humiliated and undone by the thought that they might need help to go to the bathroom or bathe. Other people can't bear the thought of their children growing up without a parent. Some cannot stand the prospect of a spouse seeing them without a breast. Some feel that if they can no longer do for others, their important others will no longer love them.

My worst fear was that I couldn't love a handicapped child. My values told me that every life is valuable, but I feared that I would hate a child who needed me to see to her most basic needs for the rest of her life. I had two good friends with seriously disabled children, and I was in awe of the time and effort they put into mothering. I also knew what an incredible strain it was for each of them. I admired them so much yet felt totally inferior to them.

I had so many hopes and dreams. I wanted to finish school, to teach, to do therapy, to write. I didn't see myself being able to have a life for myself and a life for this child. My values said, you have to give the child a chance. My biggest fear was that I was too selfish to parent this baby. I was ashamed of myself. It seemed so ugly to begrudge a disabled child anything she would need to live, but that was my worst fear. I needed to take it out and look at it, no matter how ugly it was.

Most people's worst fears are like that. We fear that when it comes down to the wire, we won't be good enough. This is where the support comes in. When you've had some support and can trust other people to help you, you gain the courage to look at these "worst fears." You may even find courage enough to speak them to another person. If the person you've chosen to tell is a true friend, the response you get is likely to be healing.

What I learned when I was able to speak my fear is that this fear is normal and human, not the reaction of a selfish monster. I found that the shame and disgust I was feeling for myself was slowly replaced with acceptance and then compassion. And with that came the strength to face whatever might happen.

Practice gratitude.

When you are anxious, your mind wants to focus on what is already wrong or what could go wrong. One of the best ways to change that focus is to remember the good that's come your way.

Take the time to enumerate the good things about the moment, the morning, the day. Stop to notice the flowers, the sunset, the smells in the air. Take a walk and notice how good it feels to be able to move. Take a nap and enjoy stretching out on your bed. Some people journal their worries, and that can help. It can also be helpful to write down what went right on a daily basis. Looking back over a week of beauty, fun, laughs, and joy can help you put your life in more balance.

With more time, you can extend your appreciation further. For me, writing notes of appreciation to people who have taught me, helped me, loved me, and befriended me always helps. I've written to friends, relatives, former teachers – even to authors I've loved but never met. Sometimes I get a response, sometimes not. Either way is OK. As I write and remember what the person did for me, I experience that pleasure again, and I work to put into words what that meant to me. When I think of the person again, he or she becomes a part of me for awhile. And I think of that person receiving the letter and knowing that he or she was appreciated. It makes me feel good to know that I could bring some joy to someone else.

Along similar lines is doing anything that brings joy to someone else. Therapist Sol Gordon calls this "mitzvah therapy." The Boy Scouts call it doing a good deed. Doing something helpful for someone else takes your mind off of you, gets you involved in doing something productive, and gives you something to feel good about.

So if you are anxious, bake a batch of cookies and take some to a neighbor. Drop in on or call someone who has been shut in. Bring flowers to work. Cook extra dinner and invite a single neighbor. Shovel your neighbor's walk when you are doing your own. If your physical energy is low or you're not able to move around very well, consider something less strenuous. Our city has a program in which people make daily calls to elderly shut-ins just to talk and make sure they are OK; there is a similar program where adults make a phone call to latch-key kids in the afternoon after school's out to make sure they got home safely, hear about their day, and help them pass the lonely time until mom or dad gets home from work. These services don't take a lot of energy, but can mean a world of difference for a lonely senior citizen or a child who is a little scared and lonely coming home to an empty house.

Doing these things for others is another way of helping yourself too. In the simplest sense, it distracts you from your worry. In the higher sense, in adding something good to the world, you shift the energy toward the positive, and this will benefit you as well as others.

—— ◆ ——

It's been almost 10 years since I learned I was pregnant. My daughter was born perfectly normal physically and mentally. She is a healthy, exuberant 9-year-old as I write this and she gives me much to laugh about and be grateful for.

Was this a miracle? I believe it was. Others say that the lab test must have been wrong. People wonder why I put myself through this uncertainty when doing other tests probably would have given me a more definitive answer. I can't really explain why I did what I did in a way that would make sense to them. I only know that I did what I felt I needed to do at the time. I prayed and I trusted my intuition. In doing that, I feel I truly did get "the highest good." Old fears were healed. I learned to dance with fear. I found my courage. This, too, is a miracle.

I would like to say that since this miracle in my life, I have never been anxious again. Unfortunately, that is not true. Life continues to throw me curves just as it does to everyone.

One of my cancer patients said that she didn't know how she could deal with cancer because it was so unpredictable; just when she thought things were OK, something new and scary would happen. I said, "Yeah, just like being a mom," and we both laughed, realizing she already had many years of experience in dealing with unpredictability.

What I can say is, I still get anxious, but I can calm down faster and stay at peace longer. When I get off balance, I can fix it more easily. I know whom to call for support, what to do for my body, and how to comfort my spirit. As with anything, practice builds skill. I was blessed with good teachers and helpful lessons along my way. I hope some of my experience might be helpful to you, and I trust that you will find your own unique way to navigate the path of your life.

The Bridge

Lisa Edwards, MBA, RD

Lisa Edwards entered into the study of clinical care with the hopes of helping others heal after her own experience of an extended hospital stay with her critically injured brother. Upon completing her undergraduate studies she began graduate work and an internship in the field of clinical nutrition. Lisa became disillusioned with a system that supported cookie-cutter recommendations and five-minute visits with patients who would go home without follow-up or support. She was motivated by the potential to change the way we deliver messages in the fields of health and wellness. She knew innately that successful intervention must be rooted in the ability to reach individuals in a way that they can uniquely appreciate.

She returned to graduate school, this time to complete a master's degree in business administration with an emphasis in marketing. Lisa completed her MBA program with honors, passed her national examination to become a Registered Dietitian, and gave birth to her first child during the winter of 1997. It was then that she began to craft the life she lives.

As an independent contractor Lisa has realized her dream of helping others through a career that turns visions into reality. She specializes in building programs that reach others with health in mind. Her life experience has shown her that perseverance amongst challenges rewards abundantly. Lisa is gifted with an ability to meet her clients wherever they might be on the spectrum of product development and grab hold to support any dimension of strategic planning, market research, development, implementation, and evaluation necessary to find fulfillment. Lisa's style emphasizes the opportunity presented by collaboration. The compilation of this book is one example of her successes.

Given Lisa's unique background combining experience as a health care and business professional, she understands that obstacles are inevitable and skillfully and persistently maneuvers the course necessary to celebrate success. She embraces the philosophy that, to be well, we must find spiritual, emotional, mental, and physical balance in our personal and professional lives. When we become whole, we realize our potential and purpose along life's path.

Lisa is blessed with the friendship and support of her husband, Dan, and three vivacious children – Abbott (6), Riley (4), and Cooper (1). They enjoy their home and community in Elk Grove, California.

Lisa Edwards, MBA, RD
healthstrategies@attbi.com
(916) 714-1683

My Story

*If you can find a path with no obstacles,
it probably doesn't lead anywhere.*
– Anonymous

Have you ever felt as if you were stranded in the middle of a bridge – unable to turn back, but afraid to move forward?

This is where I chose to spend much of the past 20 years, insisting that this was the safest place to be. I thought it was the only way to avoid the loss and pain that awaited me at either end of the bridge. Unfortunately the familiar, hollow ringing of the phone could still be heard from this solitary place.

I first recognized this haunting ring during the spring of my senior year of high school. I had spent a pivotal weekend in the Sierra Nevada Mountains with girlfriends who had grown with me from girls into women – the ones who loved me unconditionally for all they knew me to be. It was a time for friendship and laughter; however, I had an intense feeling that did not match the scene.

My heart was heavy with sadness so deep I had difficulty spending time with my friends. I often slipped away by myself, certain the angst I felt was unresolved grief. Unknown to me, I was also grieving for what was yet to come.

At the time, I believed I was grieving for my father who had died in a plane crash years earlier. I couldn't help recalling the years that had slipped by without mourning for my loss. My father died when I was barely three. The fact that I was too young to completely understand death really didn't matter because no one knew for sure that he was dead at all. After having a few drinks at a bar, he'd taken off from the local airport in his private plane. The only thing anyone knew was that he hadn't landed in any airport or open area in the Western United States. An extensive search, lasting many months, turned fear into exhaustion, but never merited mourning.

The government froze my mother's assets, assuming my father had skipped out on his family and the debt of a new business. As far as I can recall, my brothers, who were five and seven, did not cry nor did my mother when she was in front of others. She accepted my father's death early on; the man she knew would not desert his family. A few years later, she remarried and had a fourth child. My brothers and I grew, leaving behind the battlegrounds of childhood and formed friendships with each other.

My brother, my friend

It was the relationship I had with my brother Jeff that temporarily filled the hole in my heart left by my father's absence. At an age where most brothers reveled in tormenting their younger sisters, he became my protector. He was a lighthearted, handsome, and popular guy others were drawn to. Just as a father would, he made me feel that I was someone special. He was my confidant. As we grew, we would spend many late nights and long summer days listening to music, talking of dreams, and solving life's problems. At the time, these conversations were marked by innocent dreams of things we would accomplish and become.

I was eight the first time I remember "that ringing" of the phone. Of course I'd heard the phone ring before, but never like this. This sounded ominous, foreboding, as if to boast of the news it concealed. My brothers and I stared at the phone and waited while my mother listened. I didn't understand why my heart was in my throat.

A road construction crew had found a plane buried in a dense growth of trees. Pathology confirmed that the jawbone and teeth found in the wreckage were the remains of my father. The next days held news that there would be a memorial service in his honor. But my mother, brothers, and I weren't going to attend. My family felt "we had started a new life and there is no reason to go back now."

It was 14 years later during this weekend with my friends in the mountains that I finally gave myself permission to grieve. I was on the edge of being a young adult, and I longed to know this missing piece of my identity. I reveled in my sadness, but was shaken from my thoughtful place – not by the celebration, but by that same "familiar ring" that sang my name.

This time the ringing concealed the news that Jeff – my friend, my confidant, my brother – had been seriously injured. Over 70 percent of his body was covered with second- and third-degree burns. What had begun as a one-day job at the local mill to earn money for his return to college the next year ended with an emergency flight to a nearby hospital that had one of the limited number of burn centers in the country. As I rushed to be with him, my soul echoed with the words I knew to be a lie, "He'll be fine."

Many of the following days and weeks are lost in my memory. What remains were the hours of praying. I begged God to spare his life. I clung to every beep of the machine that signaled another beat of his heart. I was emotionally and physically exhausted. Unable to manage the intensity of the situation, I allowed a desperate kind of optimism to trick me into believing that every day he lived was a day closer to his recovery.

In the weeks that followed, I did not like to leave the hospital – even to avoid hearing his screams when they lowered him into the huge tanks with solution meant to cleanse his wounds. I wanted to be by his side in case he should speak. But his words came seldom, and then only to say how much he hurt or how cold he was. There was no way to tell him there wasn't enough flesh on his body to keep him warm.

As days turned into weeks, optimism gave way to denial. My family settled into a familiar routine of days at the hospital and nights at a nearby hotel during Jeff's recovery. I was easily convinced by family and friends that Jeff would be all right, and that, "he'd want me to take part in my high school graduation and go on my planned senior trip."

Five days later the familiar ringing of the phone told me that I'd given up my only chance to say goodbye. I couldn't let go of Jeff – I was consumed with the guilt I felt. It was ironic that I yearned to ask him how I would find my way out of this grief that left me wishing I were dead. How was I going to maneuver life's course without his direction and guidance? As my first independent decision, I decided not to let him go.

Living in fear of loss

During the next 10 years I searched my college campuses and every youthful hangout for someone to fill Jeff's place. His character was not to be found in the unhealthy relationships I clung to and poor choices I made. I punished myself because I believed to be happy again would dishonor Jeff's memory. Eventually I quit trying to fill these voids. Instead, I settled at the crest of the bridge – centered between loss and healing.

Somehow I muddled my way through bachelor's and master's degrees with honors. I moved on to a successful career marked by promotion every couple of years and started my own business as an independent contractor. "Independent" had become my way in more than just my professional life. No longer would I let pain touch me – independent was safe.

Somehow my life partner found me while I was operating in this "independent" mode. I suppose one of the things I found attractive in my husband was that he too was defined by his need for independence. It was a wonderful justice that he had known my brother Jeff from our childhood. He understood how deep the loss had cut me. With his support the nights of tears, marking wishful memories, lessened and eventually took on perspective. He never complained about my honest assessment that I always have a "plan B" in place – a detailed plot of how I'd move on when I lost him, or anyone else in my life.

My strategy however had one fundamental flaw: I was overwhelmed with the love I felt for the first two children that resulted from my marriage. Now pregnant with my third, I struggled with the intensity of my need for my children and lived every day in fear I would lose them. No matter how I tried I couldn't concoct a "plan B." I convinced myself that I'd already carried my share of misfortune. I pushed the fear of loss down as I struggled to manage my love. Then it came – the same torturous ring of the phone, "Mrs. Edwards, this is Dr. Hershey's office. Is your husband with you?"

If born alive, it appeared my son whom we named Matthew Isaiah, was destined for a shortened life, punctuated with serious health issues. Loss and fear had found me once again, by stealing the life of my stillborn baby. I felt betrayed by my love for my other two children. But that very love is what forced me out of bed each morning. As much as I wanted to die and be free of the persistent pain, I couldn't leave them emotionally or physically, as my father, brother and son had left me.

I did not delay the grieving process this time. There was no denying the nursery was as empty as my womb. My arms ached to hold Matthew and the only relief came from caring for my other two children. Each morning I rose, resolved not to let another hour go by – another second – longing for what was lost, while missing the blessings of today. If I were on earth for the love of my children, then I would revel in the glory that my son was living with Christ in wholeness and health.

It's been two years since I held Matthew in my arms. My fourth child recently turned one. He epitomizes the hope for new life and new beginnings as he runs to keep up with his older brother and sister. This past year has been marked by fresh starts – a new home, a new office, the first day of kindergarten, the first day of preschool, the first loose tooth – first steps for us all.

On either side of here to there

In all the uncertainty, I found the strength to uncover the stepping stone hidden by Matthew's ashes. Now I can see those other stepping stones that preceded Matthew's along my path – those worn smooth at the center from lingering too long. I see the moss that has finally been allowed to grow and soften the sharp edges and I find comfort. My triumphs have given me a renewed spirit as I face the reality that the phone may very well ring again. For as I close the cover on my losses and arrange them in my overflowing bookshelves, I realize there are chapters yet to be written. I accept life with new faith, learning that to live is to believe that my days on this earth are numbered. I find comfort in knowing that one day I will embrace those I didn't get to hold nearly long enough on this earth.

My love for my husband holds unlimited possibilities as I learn to focus on the blessings of today. I *have* been blessed with friendship marked by respect, protection, and conversations filled with innocent dreams of things to come. I now realize that while for most of my life I stood at the crest of the bridge, I did not always stand alone.

My business and those I serve continue to grow and fulfill in a way I had been unable to describe until recent conversation with a new friend. I told her of my business and offered that I realize my success in taking the ideas and passions of others and finding a way to make them into a reality. I told her that I feel most successful when I am able to find new synergy and bring together those who did not see the common ground.

"You're a bridge," she said. I laughed inside with the thought of the independent stance I'd held for so long, thinking the label would never fit. "I'm too independent," I replied. Then I was struck with new awareness. A bridge must stand independent if it is to be able to connect what lies on either side.

I realize now the bridge that had held me emotionally bound for so many years had actually offered a gift of vision. Through the independence I sought, I learned to forgo the comfort found in walking the well-traveled paths. From the crest in the bridge where I stood, I'd learned to seek the limitless possibilities that lie on either side of here to there.

The Bridge

Bridging the gap

> *Do not follow where the path may lead.*
> *Go instead where there is no path and leave a trail.*
> – Ralph Waldo Emerson

I no longer think of the bridge as holding me captive, just as I have come to realize that we are powerless if we try to cross it alone. Taking the stance at the middle of the bridge and bringing together that which lies on either side requires a willingness to go it alone mixed with the ability to walk with others. I believe that each of us has the strength to bridge gaps if we are willing to take the chance. I encourage you to seek the role you are meant to play in finding common purpose.

- *Understand that while it is your dream, everyone deserves to see it realized.* We are all given special gifts, and the role we play in this world is unique. Don't let your personal contribution go unfelt by convincing yourself that no one else cares.

- *Realize that you are not alone.* There is someone else out there who appreciates your vision, although they may not know it yet. Identify those who might see the benefits and opportunities presented by your ideas.

- *Make the connection.* Contact each of these people. Explain where your interest comes in and then share why you think they might also be interested. Remember your goals don't have to be the same – just complementary.

- *Persist in the vision.* All too often great ideas are lost to a lack of persistence. After finding partners in the endeavor, you must have the perspective to take the lead and see the vision through to reality.

- *Always have a "plan B."* Your vision may be reshaped with the wisdom and insight of others who care. Be flexible and be ready to try again if the first efforts don't turn out the way you would have hoped. Keep in mind that alternate outcomes may meet similar goals.

- *Keep your eye on all the possibility that life holds.* Finding your path and walking it with others is harder than walking alone – yet so much more fulfilling. Don't let setbacks or obstacles take attention away from all the possibilities in life. Keep your vision strong and accept the innate wisdom that you have a unique gift and role in this world. The sum of our collective successes depends on those who are strong enough to bridge the distance from here to there.

We are all angels that only have one wing
All angels searching for each other
We are all angels who cannot touch the sky
Because we need each other to fly

– Songwriters Karen Drucker and Michael Gott

My wish for us all is that we will seek the possibility, take the chance, find the synergy, and make the difference!

Finding Authentic Happiness
in the Chaos of Life

Donna Allen, PhD, MS Ed, CHES, FAWHP

Donna Allen finds authentic happiness from the joy and gratification she receives from serving and teaching others. She is a single parent of three young children. Life experiences have provided her the opportunity to recognize the beauty and immeasurable strength of the spirit and zest for living.

She has made over 100 presentations and has been an invited keynoter to numerous conferences, presenting to diverse audiences around the United States. Her gift is inspiration. She will inspire you to love yourself, forgive, be gentle with the past, and to carry along the unpredictable pathways of life essentials including laughter, love, and compassion for self and others.

From 1989-91 she was the number one female collegiate cyclist in the Southwest United States while road racing for Baylor University in Waco, Texas. She competed for a spot on the women's 1992 Barcelona cycling team at Olympic Training Centers in Lake Placid and Colorado Springs. She believes that her spirit, hopefulness, perseverance, and determination allowed her to reach her athletic potential.

Through these experiences she's reminded of the actions required to move along the pathways of life.

As an Associate Professor and Director of the Center for Health Promotion at Emporia State University, Emporia, Kansas, Donna has earned prestigious professional recognition for her excellence in teaching including Kansas Health Educator of the Year, University Teacher of the Year, and the Excellence in Teaching Award. In 2003 she was awarded the Innovation in Teaching Award, one of the highest honors bestowed on a faculty member at Emporia State University. She is a Certified Health Education Specialist (CHES) and Fellow of the Association for Worksite Health Promotion (FAWHP).

Her passion is serving as a mentor and teacher to her children and college students.

Donna and her three children, Cade (7), Casey (6), and Cale (3) live with two cats, Merval and Skidmark. Donna loves her children and still follows her passion for long-distance cycling.

Donna Allen, PhD, MS Ed, CHES, FAWHP
1417 West Street
Emporia, KS 66801
allendon@esumail.emporia.edu
www.emporia.edu/hper/faculty/allen/home.htm

My Story

Life is what happens between your plans

Seven shoes by the door. Only seven. To function in the morning, the minimal requirement at our house is eight. Eight shoes. One for each tiny foot for the cushioning of the soul. To utterly function with social conventionality, there must be eight shoes. Every soul must be covered before we leave the door. There's no way around it. We must search. And so the search begins.

In a proactive sense, if everyone would just put their shoes by the door, geared up for the action that is required by stepping out into the world, there might be some readiness. But then again, life doesn't always go as planned.

We all could perhaps be more cognizant of protecting our souls. Walking out into strange worlds without protection can be dangerous. Yet, as we soul search, we sometimes allow our distractions – for me, I call them internal thoughts of my own inadequacies, low self-esteem, emotional baggage of a dysfunctional past, and tragic circumstances – to absolutely stop us dead in our tracks.

Pathway of hope and courage

If someone had outlined for me what I would face in my life, I might have concluded that I was incapable of surviving these hellacious and chaotic pathways. At birth I weighed 3 pounds, delivered two months early and received a complete blood transfusion while my mom severally hemorrhaged. Seven days after I was born, my father raped my mother who was still recovering in the hospital from a difficult birth and broke her breastbone.

Later I was told as an infant that my father, in uncontrollable anger, would bang me against the wall until blood ran out my nose and ears. Fortunately, I don't remember but am thankful for survival. I still struggle with the horror of it but triumph in forgiveness. Mine is the story of hope and courage. It is the pathway I choose. It helps me over-come uncontrollable grief and move on to help others in my life.

Unpredictability, seasoned regularly with anger and yelling, was our home life. School wasn't much easier. I was one of the poor kids. Everyone knew because poor kids were the ones with the pink free-lunch tickets. Kids can be so cruel. I carried the label of a "have not" through high school. This belief was reinforced on multiple fronts including home, school, and society. Such unkindness was a perfect segue to those things I sometimes struggle with today: feelings of unworthiness for a better life.

I am unable to put into words how natural it seemed to grow up with very little or no self-worth given my day-to-day grind and dysfunc-tional circumstances. As I look back, I see the substantial amount of energy I was obviously blessed with to withstand this abuse, while taking on the responsibility for the safety and care of my younger brother, 11 months younger to be exact, and, to the best of my ability, protecting my mother from my father's harsh verbal and physical abuse. I was the rebel, the one at 2 a.m. who advocated clearly "please let us go to sleep now" and would, as you can imagine, be put right back into place by my dad.

As I reflect on this season of life, I acknowledge myself for the energy and will to survive. Perhaps a rebel, more importantly, a strong and spirited person.

"He will never be back"

My husband and I had been married for five years after dating for three years. One morning, I awoke to find a gift from him on the table. An "I love you" note accompanied by a complete screenplay from the Wizard of Oz, truly a favorite to this Kansas native. I was living life as heaven on earth.

As I reveled in this act of kindness I proceeded to go about my daily chores. The chocolate syrup, spilled in the refrigerator weeks ago, had become somewhat of a difficult challenge. Then, the phone rang. My husband had been in a serious car accident. I drove in a trance to a hospital 77 miles away not knowing the severity of this pathway in my life.

A nightmare, turned real. How could this be real? This wasn't part of the plan. I was living life at a time when we were actually carrying out the "happily ever after" part. Chaos, OK, but not THIS.

Slowly he worked to regain memory, thought, and physical and mental functioning through physical, speech, and occupational therapy. For every gain made in physical healing, there was reason for celebration. Little did we know.

Anyone who has gone through traumatic brain injury or experienced it, whether as a caregiver, victim, or survivor, has gotten as close to death as is allowed. Each brain injury is unique. For us, the final outcome, which evolves through years of bittersweet physical healing, was an emotionally altered person who was dangerous for my children and myself. It took years and years for the neuropsychologist and therapists' message to register with me, "Your husband died in a car accident, and he will never be back." His body, was functioning, but the man I married had died.

Eventually, after years of support during this trauma and going to all extremes and exhausting all possibilities to save my marriage, I had to choose survival, purely for the safety and well-being of myself and my children. The loving man I married was gone, and the person who emerged was angry, paranoid, and verbally abusive.

He was stalking me and constantly calling. One evening in his anger he almost backed over our 2-year-old. I remember darting behind the car to rescue my toddler while calling out to the neighbor. This was sickening. I felt threatened. I needed shelter and support.

With the help of my therapist, I took a big step. I allowed others to take care of me. I appreciated the guidance I received from so many supportive women in this never-ending darkness.

The time spent in the women's shelter with my three toddlers was one of the most absolute desperate and sad times of my life. Where do I go from here? How do I ever go home? I was leaving the shelter, going to work, and returning to the shelter. While I was thankful to have a safe haven, I was devastated by this lifestyle. I felt so helpless, and deeply sorry for my children. It seemed as if the pathway that lay before me was a downward spiral, and I needed all my energy just to cling to the responsibilities of life and keep my family safe. I can't describe the feeling of walking into my boss's office and telling him I was staying at the shelter, that I felt my work was suffering, and that I was so sorry not to be able to work to my full capacity. I can't convey the pure exhaustion and perceived complete deterioration of my life.

I knew, without a doubt, that my spirit had been broken. My strong Olympic spirit. Absolutely broken. Into many, many pieces. My strength and spirit was gone . . . lost. Yet, here I sit, drawing my breath in gratitude for the opportunities that arose from my circumstances.

I am so thankful for these opportunities. Suddenly like angels in my pathway were women – strong encouraging women, the most kind and dignified women you will ever find – who work day in and day out with abused women to help and support the rebuilding of life pathways. They chose to help me carry my burdens and ever so slowly and gently pick me up and help me recognize that I must carry on. On this path, I was exposed to the purest support, empathy, and kindness that I have ever known. There is so much strength that we can give to one another through what seems to be an elementary, yet genuine care and concern for others.

Amidst the calamity, chaos, uncertainty, and pure stress of these circumstances were rays of hope, authentic hope, offered to me by caregivers, physicians, therapists, friends, coworkers, and family.

A thousand tears

Like wildflowers bravely growing defiantly through the cracks of a sidewalk, I have chosen to live, bloom, and forgive. I have chosen to hope again. I have chosen to move forward on these pathways. Through these journeys I have experienced authentic happiness. I sit here in tears as I relate this newfound principle, because it has taken my whole life, and I still struggle, to allow myself the opportunity to feel the value of happiness and joy in my life. Along the pathway of life, I have learned that I am worthy and deserving of authentic happiness and joy. It's a process to learn to be greater than your pain.

Could I cry a thousand tears? Indeed. Sometimes I still do. Very few days go by that I don't think to myself, "What if? What if my past had been different? Could my life have been more normal?" And we all have a definition of normal. Sometimes, there is a feeling that will just weaken me and draw me to my knees. I am at times sad because of my past, and even present moments, but the overriding sorrow comes from the outpouring of support and love I have received from my closest and truest friends that extends past and is stronger than any pain I have lived through. I am unable sometimes to understand that there are people who care for **me**.

I have also discovered that it is OK for me to care for me. Taking on the role of caregiving is a natural role because my children are young, and I am a full-time university professor caring for others day and night. I have discovered it is much more familiar for me to cushion the souls of others than to take care of and protect myself.

Living in chaos is much more familiar to me than calm. It is a process, perhaps an enlightening of my spirit, that who I am and what I am is worthwhile to others in my world.

Life is that thing that happens between plans. What I want is to be a light to you and others in this peculiar thing called life. All of us need to find those "things" to cushion our steps through life, and use our strengths. Sometimes we must allow others to carry our burdens and take our steps with us. This is what we are called to do. Simply love one another. And always give thanks.

Unfinished business

Did I plan to be a single parent with three young ones? No. The experiences I have had with living and then moving on from the loss of my husband to traumatic brain injury have been significant crossroads in my path of life. When all that you have hoped for has changed, life can seem like an endless nightmare, an eternal period of blackness. Each one of us, if required, can recall past experiences that have been traumatic, painful, and unforgettable. This type of unfinished business has the potential to hang on and rot you to the cold, cold core of your being. I applaud and admire many who seemingly have no unfinished business with the past. But if you do, I give you this advice.

Forgive. If you have trouble with this, and believe me, sometimes it is easier said than done, allow yourself to ponder this option. But let me give you a gift, listen carefully: Forgive yourself. You may not be at a point in your life to forgive the wrong doings or circumstances imposed in your life by the actions of others or yourself. But you can forgive yourself. Forgive yourself for holding on to those acidic and pungent feelings for such a long time. And when you do, acknowledge your strengths and joys. Discover the joy of authentic happiness, those little things that allow you to celebrate life. Even if it is just breathing. Some pathways require baby steps. And each step in a direction of security and release of anguish is great in itself.

Sometimes there is so much to carry and, as we move through our seasons of life, we must learn or perhaps relearn to sift through these experiences and never tire of searching for hope. Hope to carry on and sense contentment and peace from doing so. Without hope and courage sprinkled with optimism and thankfulness for a better day, life can be very demanding.

Finding Authentic Happiness in the Chaos of Life

Preparing for pathways

Over and over again we are called upon to start a new life, down a new pathway. I don't know if a person ever truly overcomes loss, but we can survive. And in the surviving there can be healing. And from this healing comes learning. We learn what to carry with us. And we take this and then, ever so slowly, we move on. Finally, moving on to help others.

I attribute much of my success to enduring life circumstances. Without my particular life experiences, I would not have experienced the authentic joy of friendship, the support of family, and the everlasting spirit that we all have to merely survive. While day-to-day survival is certainly a personal goal, I have simultaneously and carefully chosen to allow these stumbling blocks to shape and reshape my character and have used them to learn, to move on, and to move on to help others.

I began a traumatic brain injury support group three years ago to help others in my community. I attend a support group at the women's shelter where I continue to learn and grow and to help others. I serve my family. And while doing so, I remember to put on my own oxygen mask and breathe. Breathe in and let my breaths carry me.

If you're going though hell, keep going

I am living proof that there is strength of the spirit. More strength than pain can ever be. That raw courage can move you past fear of the future and the acidity of life. Courage is taking reasonable risks for a good cause, standing up for what you believe, standing up for the rights of others, and being who you are regardless of others' opinions.

Courage does not have to be an ostentatious or superhuman feat. It can be as simple as getting up each day, telling yourself that your life counts and is worth living, and then living life in whatever state of mind you find yourself in. This is courage.

I have experienced life with a broken spirit. I have experienced breath moving through my body while walking in living death. More importantly, I have survived and actively discovered the spirit to be the zest of life, the hope and foundation for moving on. There was a time in my life when this spirit was absolutely broken. While in this state, I recognized the desperation of life without hope and energy, joy, faith, peace, and contentment. May I, in my wildest nightmares, never again be confronted with anything like this again. Yet, there is no guarantee. What I have learned from tragedy is that we can move forward through chaos. If you are going through hell, keep going.

Undefined pathways

One thing is certain. Life holds mysterious and magical pathways. Incidents may very well turn your world upside down. Again, the opportunity to live through hell is significant. Each day I struggle with three strong-willed children, undone homework, overflowing laundry baskets, toys in the neighbor's yard, soccer and basketball practice, a house that is simply not self-cleaning, and late nights silently sobbing over my keyboard at overwhelming responsibilities.

Look beyond, through, and in between the chaos of your life. The chaos will always be present. Slowly, like a sunset, I am learning that I can survive. And from the surviving, live. And in my living, extend a hand to others. It is my choice to give thanks for all things life has taught me.

If you struggle on your pathway, with your heart, reach out your hand. Allow others to know about and carry your burdens. If you have a hand to extend, do so willingly to help another. This may seem an uncomplicated message, but is so much easier said than done. As we grow old – rather older – there will be more loss. And the heart will need attention and healing. On some pathways, your hope may wane, but draw on your strengths and courage. At the lowest of times, remember the heart is so fragile because it has known the full spectrum of love. Each time there is opportunity for devastation, there is opportunity for growth. But it doesn't happen overnight.

Over and over again we are called upon to start a new life, a new pathway. For each journey we must find our shoes, protect our souls and bring with us those things that will carry us through. Fall in love with the strengths you have to carry you on your pathway. It's best to keep your shoes, all of them, by the door When possible on your journey, carry your weather and strengths with you. This is the best way to cushion your soul with the happiness you deserve.

Seven shoes by the door. Don't ever stop searching for your shoes. It is hard to search. And when, not if, you discover the placements of your protections, you will step out in stride. Through this laborious process you will grow. In some situations, know that barefoot may be the most comfortable way to travel. Be ready to step out on your pathway. When the storms come, know that you have the protection you need, or hold the hope that you will have the courage to find whatever you need along your path.   On occasion, we must dance in the rain.

God bless.

My Second Act

Betty Auchard

Betty Auchard is a native of Iowa and lived in the Midwest until 1956. When her husband, Denny, became a member of the faculty of San Jose State University in San Jose, California, the family relocated permanently to the West Coast. She raised four children, became a grandmother of nine, earned a teaching credential, and eventually taught high school art.

Betty's fiber arts – batik, nature printing on fabric and paper, and handspun wools dyed with plants – have been included in periodicals such as *Threads* magazine and such books as *Leaf Printing on Fabric* by Jean Ray Laury and *Making Journals by Hand* by Jason Thompson.

After her husband died in 1998, writing became Betty's tool for healing and eventually took on a life of its own. Many of her memoir stories have been published in the Chocolate for a Woman's Soul series, anthologies by Simon & Schuster, and will eventually appear in her own collection titled *My Second Act*. She's also writing about her experiences growing up poor in Iowa in the 1930s.

In addition to writing full-time, Betty has been a public speaker since May 2002 presenting the humorous, inspiring story of her book to groups and organizations in the Bay Area of California. *My Second Act* tells of her adventures and misadventures while learning how to be single at 68 when she had never been single before. She feels that after suffering a loss, surviving and thriving are necessary for recovery and should be celebrated.

Contact Betty for information regarding presentations or a CD of Betty reading 14 poignant and funny stories from *My Second Act.*

Betty Auchard
115 Belhaven Dr.
Los Gatos, CA 95032
(408) 356-8224
btauchard@aol.com
www.bettyauchard.com

My Story

Whenever I learn that a friend has lost a spouse or significant other, my heart aches. I know what lies ahead for her because losing a long-time partner is a life-altering experience. When my good friend's husband was dying of cancer, she and I kept in close touch by email since she lived over a thousand miles away. I knew that any time of the day or night she might need someone to talk to. After she became a widow, I was her primary support system.

"Grieving is pure hell," she wrote. "Betty, I don't know how you got through it."

I never consciously thought about how I got through grief, but my gut had told me that I couldn't avoid the pain that was ahead. People are supposed to die and those left behind are supposed to feel sad. So I waded through my bereavement the only way I knew – which was head on. I cried when I felt like it and laughed whenever I could. I never stopped moving and prayed all the time. My daily plea was, "God, please keep me afloat."

What helped even more than praying was having someone to listen as I babbled on and on. I talked endlessly, and only those who understood tolerated it. By retelling the events of Denny's death, I was finally able to absorb the reality of my loss. I missed him so much that it took a long time before I got used to the fact that he was gone for good and that my life would never be the same again.

I joined a support group, which may not be for everyone, but it helped me. I didn't mind crying with others as we shared our sadness, regrets, and sometimes anger. It touched me to see a man in my group weeping over the loss of his wife, regretting that he had never learned to do the laundry or cook his own eggs. Another man had never written a check because his wife took care of the finances.

I also spent each evening reading and crying my way through bereavement books as I wrote in the margins. It was like having a dialogue with the author, which was another way of talking to someone. During the day, I was so forgetful and preoccupied with memories that I couldn't remember much of anything else. When I had jobs to do, I wrote them down on a list and then couldn't find the list. I felt heavy and dragged myself through each day. My appetite was missing and so was my brain. I felt disengaged. Driving a car was risky business, and I almost caused an accident twice. At night, I often drove for miles with the headlights off until a more alert driver gave me the "horn."

But what helped me most of all was concentrating on something that gave me comfort, which was writing down my thoughts. You might find comfort in gardening, cooking, or service to others. But for me, writing gave me solace, and every day I jotted down the thoughts and feelings that filled my heart. Sometimes the reflections were heartbreaking – sometimes they were resentful. I wrote on whatever was handy: scraps of paper, backs of envelopes, receipts, or anything that would take the mark of a pen. I put the little pieces of paper in safe places, but I never remembered where those places were.

Gradually, I abandoned scribbling on scraps and used full-sized sheets of paper. The notes became paragraphs, pages, and then chapters. Writing began as my tool for healing and eventually became my passion.

Now that I'm finally cleaning out drawers and cupboards that haven't been touched for several years, I'm finding those notes. I don't even remember writing some of them. But they bring back memories of my passage through grief, a journey that I marked with stories I would like to share with you.

My Second Act

My donations: Embracing the pain

I wrap my feelings in funny words and give them away so you might listen and hear my heart through my paragraphs on paper, for that's how I package my pain. I have more than I want and have used what I need. I like to share, so please enjoy or pass the pain along to someone else. Avoid calling Goodwill; they won't pick it up, for pain's not deductible. Someday it **might** be when there's too much discomfort for humanity to bear. We'll hide our emotions, disguise them as knick-knacks, and Goodwill won't know they're collecting bags of sorrow labeled as "useful" and left on the porch to be picked up by noon.

But until that happens, I'll conceal my hurting inside the polite wrapping of smart, funny writing that makes others crack up and fall on the hard floor and lie there a-laughing. It's the way I get rid of my pain.

Negotiations have ended: Accepting the loss

After several months of being a widow, I sensed I had regained a fragment of my stability. I still cried when I felt like it, but I was learning to stay afloat. Three times in a row I paid the bills on time and did all I could to follow Denny's master budget plan. But I wanted to do more than just follow the leader, so feeling plucky, I decided to make some changes on my own. The familiar things around me that we had shared for almost 49 years were a constant, painful reminder that he was gone. Meeting widowhood head on, I started replacing our belongings.

The first thing to go was our massive dark walnut bedroom furniture. Alone, I was lost on that half-acre of king-sized mattress. My daughter and her husband, who lived with an odd assortment of furniture, took all six pieces. It was their first bedroom set, and they were thrilled to have it. The room where I had slept with Denny for decades was now empty.

I moved into the computer room, sleeping on a day bed at night and shopping each day for a bedroom set of my own. After many weeks of searching, I found a charming Shaker style that I adored, and it was on sale. I put strips of masking tape on the floor and walls of the bedroom, pretending it was furniture. It fit, so I ordered every piece and left town for two weeks on my first trip without Denny.

While I was watching two live shows a day in Branson, Missouri, my children were at home painting the master bedroom and bath with my all-time favorite non-color, Kelly Moore Navajo white. The furniture arrived while I was away, and my family set all six pieces in their designated places. When I returned to my new nest, with the bed freshly made and nothing on the walls but what I might put there, I felt that I had taken the first steps in starting my life over.

That night, while flossing my teeth in the newly painted bathroom, I noticed the gray front tooth that had always bugged me despite the fact that Denny never noticed it. Even my 80-year-old mother in the convalescent home, who had cataracts, had asked, "Is your front tooth kinda gray or are my eyes gettin' worse?"

Denny insisted, "I never even notice that dark tooth, honey. Forget about it."

But I never did, and I wanted that ugly tooth out of my face. With very little thought about the master budget plan, I made an appointment the next day to have my four front teeth capped, then pondered what I might do next. There were many things on our master list, but Denny and I couldn't agree on what should come first, so our life-improvement projects often bogged down during negotiations.

I wanted double pane windows; he wanted new carpets. I wanted new copper pipes; he wanted a new car. I wanted a cell phone, email service, and an ATM card; but he didn't want any of those things and declared, "Honey, that stuff isn't necessary." Just thinking about what I could do on my own brightened my mood significantly because I could do what I wanted without negotiating.

"Without negotiating."

The words shot through my heart and ripped it open. While staring at the gray front tooth that I was about to replace, I wept with sorrow because negotiations had ended . . . forever.

Millennium: Learning to live without the person

I had finally gotten used to the word *millennium* in everyday conversation when the phrase "Y2K" entered the scene. It had a catchy sound and look. But no one knew how long it took me to figure out what it meant. I was alone, thank God, when I realized it meant "Year Two Thousand." I said aloud to myself, "Oh, yeah. I get it." But I realized I still had more to learn when someone asked, "Betty, are you Y2K compliant?"

The new phrase was plastered everywhere in big, colorful letters. It began to worry me. One night, a newscaster asked from the television screen, "Are you Y2K compliant?" I grabbed a strand of hair, twisted it in my fingers, and whimpered, "I don't know."

Media coverage made matters worse. It warned of complexities regarding bank account numbers, documents, and records because of snags involving zeros and the number nine. It was far too complex to understand, and I had no idea what to do about it. I only knew that I wasn't prepared for what the year 2000 might bring.

Should I stash some cash, fill my tank with gas, have plenty of food, water, and medical supplies available, and maybe a flashlight? I expected looting and vandalism. My garage was too full of junk to make room for my car, so I worried that it could be in big trouble, unprotected in the driveway. It felt as if the end of the world were coming instead of a new century.

It did not help matters that I would enter the year 2000 alone, without Denny beside me. He had planned a milestone celebration because the century would change on the heels of our 50th anniversary. It was a wonderful coincidence – but it wasn't meant to be. Denny had a date with cancer instead of with the millennium and me.

The foreboding news of possible vandalism and looting didn't help my frame of mind either. It filled me with dread, and I felt more alone than ever in my new role as a widow. I declined New Year's Eve parties to stay home and guard my house and car – and watch the world fall apart on television from the safety of my bed. I felt weepy as I crawled beneath the down comforter alone and thought of Denny.

The television coverage was magnificent as it showed New Year celebrations and pageantry around the world. It was a welcome distraction. I was glad to see the mayhem hadn't yet started in other countries, but maybe only America expected chaos.

As I flipped from channel to channel watching the nations of the world enter the new century, I forgot to worry. Soon, I was too weary to witness the arrival of the year 2000 on TV, so I turned out the light and hunkered under the covers. I prayed that my street would be the same in the morning and my car would remain in the driveway, unharmed. I was so tired from fretting that I easily fell asleep.

I had slept less than an hour when I was awakened by what I thought was the sound of popcorn popping in my microwave. I sat upright with eyes bulging. Had revelers invaded my kitchen? I picked up the phone to call for help and noticed the time. It was 12:05 a.m. New Year's Day. I cautiously peeked out the window. My car was still there. No one was in the streets; there were no sparklers, drunkards, or anything.

No lions or tigers or bears. Oh, my.

Hearing the faint sound of firecrackers in the distance, I was reassured the house had not been overtaken by corn-popping prowlers. A few minutes later it was over.

I said aloud, "Is that all there is? Where is everybody?" I had expected more than that in the way of celebration and hell-raising for a new century. I was so relieved. My whole body felt different. I had come through the front door of the Year Two Thousand alone and unharmed. I felt like Wonder Woman.

I crawled back under the comfort of down, fell asleep, and dreamed. I was ready for Y2K. *Anything* was now possible.

The carpet man: Reinvesting emotional energy

A few years after Denny died, I got a crush on the carpet man. I knew then that I must be moving on.

In the middle of home improvements, I had dashed to the rug mart wearing grubby work clothes, old sneakers, and no lipstick to have a quick look at area rugs. The man who waited on me was a nice look-ing guy with slightly gray curly hair, twinkling eyes, and a laugh like jazzy music. I had so much fun with him that I began to consider more than just a rug for my home. I pondered which chair he might use when we watched a movie together. After that first meeting, I couldn't stop smiling all the way home and resolved to look better the next time I sought his advice.

I sought his advice the very next day, but this time I dressed for the occasion, complete with bright red toenails, a toe ring, and my best-looking sandals. To bring attention to my strategically placed foot as we studied rug samples, I tapped it on the floor and gushed, "Now THAT'S a nice lookin' rug."

I discussed flooring with him often and became known as "his" customer. As his customer, I started wearing eye makeup and nice clothes. But I was self-conscious about the wattle under my chin. It made me look old. If he stood to my left as we talked, I would pretend to be thinking about rug stuff by holding my left hand casually under my chin to hide my wattle. If he stood to my right, I hid the wattle with my right hand. It was a lot of work and, for the first time in my life, I considered having that wattle removed. I made a mental note to do some research in the yellow pages.

One time I called to say, "Carpet Man, I'm going to be gone for seven days, but I'll see you next week."

He was in a goofy mood and affected an exaggerated southern accent, saying, "Betty, Ahm so sahrry that y'all won't be comin' in today. Ah was so lookin' forward to seein' y'all. Mah heart will jus' be pinin' for ya 'til next week." That silly southern accent got me so excited that I considered carpeting the garage, the driveway, and the sidewalk. But a new kitchen floor seemed more practical.

I had never in my life had a hare-brained flirtation like that, but it made me feel alive again. I was like a 16-year-old girl and all because of a guy who laughed a lot. We laughed so much that I was afraid he might get in trouble. "Carpet Man, your boss is going to think we're crazy," I cautioned.

With a wave of his hand he said, "Hey, we're consenting adults over 21 and can do what we want."

"Consenting adults over 21?" Thank goodness his ring finger was bare. It meant I could flirt forever. If he had asked me out for coffee or even mud wrestling, I was so smitten that I would have gone in a minute.

But nothing like that ever happened.

I was busy for 12 months upgrading one floor after another and everything was looking better because of my crush on the carpet man. I bought all new brass floor vents and carpeted the hall, stairs, and master bedroom. I had every scrap of carpet bound and had to hunt for places to use all those little rugs. I replaced the vinyl in three bathrooms and took out a home improvement loan to upgrade the kitchen so I could have laminate flooring installed. I stalked the carpet man for a whole year, but we never even went out for coffee because the only thing in my home that got his attention was the floor.

I'm not sorry. Apparently his "real" job was to open my heart, and he certainly did that. After the carpet man, I was ready to live and love again. And my house has never looked better.

My grief is a memory: Grief pressed stories from my heart, and poems that made me cry. Now, almost five years later, human pleasures and earthly places are teasing me and filling my heart with hope. Am I glad? Oh, yeah, I'm glad.

The Garden

The garden beckons,
and warm days remind me
that two seasons have passed
since I last touched plants.

I ignored my roses,
hydrangeas and pansies
and stayed inside
to write away my pain.

I forgot the joy of planting,
but now I remember:
I loved grooming old plants
and pampering new ones.

The garden flourished
two springs ago
when I lived all day
in my blue jeans and sweat.

It feels so good
to get my hands dirty
and pull weeds again
in the loamy, wormy soil.

– Betty Auchard

Choose Life, Choose Happiness

Rachel Hall and Renita Freeman

Rachel Hall is the Director of Clinical Research for TCI Medical™, a small medical innovation company. Prior to her current role, she spent 16 years in the corporate world as a top-notch financial analyst and computer system specialist. After being diagnosed with breast cancer four years ago, she has taken steps to help make a difference with regard to early detection of breast cancer.

She formed the company Hall HealthMax, LLC, with the purpose of educating women on early detection. She then volunteered with TCI Medical™ testing a new breast cancer detection device, with no compression or radiation, in clinical trials. Now she is a key executive helping to develop this device and bring it to market. The process of getting regulatory approval in the US and Europe is ongoing as of this writing.

Rachel Hall
Hall HealthMax, LLC, and TCI Medical™
rhall@tcimed.com
www.tcimed.com

Renita Freeman is a freelance writer and health care researcher. She is currently working with the Technology Center for Cancer Research, Inc., a nonprofit organization supporting new technology and research for the early detection of cancer. Additionally, she is writing a variety of articles that focus on health and safety issues, and human interest stories showcasing people who are making a positive difference in their lives and the lives of others.

Renita has two children, Danae and Dustin, who have been the light in her life and have often served as an inspiration for her freelance writing. She makes her home in the Rocky Mountains of New Mexico where she loves to spend her time playing music, taking photographs, and writing her stories.

Renita Freeman
Freeman Freelance, LLC
PO Box 459
Tijeras, NM 87059
freelanc@swcp.com
www.tccr.nm.org

The Story

Lives collide in the most serendipitous ways. And in that collision can lie transformation, renewal, and hope. Not many people can pinpoint a specific incident that changed the path of their lives. However, that's not the case for Rachel Hall and Renita Freeman. Rachel's path started to change after a diagnosis of breast cancer. Renita's path changed after meeting Rachel's husband, Russell, and hearing their story of recovery. Both women found hope and renewal for their lives, especially after meeting each other. Isn't it funny how meeting one person can transform the path of your life? Enjoy the intricate web life weaves.

Renita Freeman: How many of us go through our lives with little thought to the questions, "Am I really happy? Am I living my life the way I want to be living it?" How many of us even give thought to,

"Am I even **living**? Am I **choosing** life, or am I just getting by day to day?"

All too often we operate on autopilot without giving any thought to these questions. For many of us, it's only when we have a near-fatal accident or are diagnosed with a life-threatening illness that we stop to look at our lives and the possibility that we won't live forever. We suddenly find ourselves wanting to hang on to our lives more than ever, remembering that we once felt passionate about our dreams. As women, we let ourselves get caught up in "because I'm supposed to" instead of "because it's good for me," and we find ourselves in a mediocre or unfulfilling life that we never intended for ourselves.

Two years ago, that was me. I was just trying to get through each day. I was running to work, running errands, running, running, running away from life – until someone unintentionally caught my attention. I found myself looking at my life and taking stock. I didn't like what I saw.

I was approaching my ninth year of marriage. Just staying married, for me, seemed like an accomplishment in and of itself, when so many couples were throwing in the towel. It hadn't been an easy nine years. Deep down I knew I wasn't happy, but I was trying to convince myself it was better to stay with the familiar, rather than face the dating game at 44 or, what seemed worse, being alone.

My health had been in decline over the past two years. I had gone from strong and healthy, to tired and overweight, catching everything from cold and flu bugs to more mysterious and serious illnesses. A myriad of physicians shuffled me from one specialist to another. I underwent test after test while still declining rapidly – physically, mentally, emotionally, and spiritually.

I had this nagging feeling that if I didn't make some drastic changes in my life, I would literally die soon. I was a workaholic desperately trying to keep up with the bills my husband kept creating – always feeling that it was my responsibility. I was so caught up with what I thought I was **supposed** to do, it hadn't occurred to me I could live any other way. That is, until the evening I met Russell Hall, the husband of a very special woman.

He was a quiet man, his office three doors down from mine. I met him briefly during my first week at a new job. During a staff meeting, I had been "volunteered" to organize the company's annual participation in the American Cancer Society's fund-raising walk. I thought, "Great, just what I need, one more thing on my plate."

One evening on his way out, this kind man whom I'd never really spoken to, stopped in my office to donate money for the walk and let me know he and his wife would be participating. He wanted to know if he could help in any other way. His wife, he told me, was a recent survivor of breast cancer, and he appreciated my willingness to organize the company's participation. I immediately felt guilty for silently feeling I was "too busy" to participate.

When he mentioned his wife's cancer, there was something in his expression that made me say how very sorry I was to learn that cancer had touched his life personally. He surprised me by sitting down and taking time to tell me "their" story of surviving cancer. He talked about his wife, Rachel, and how she had to push for a mammogram after finding the lump and push again to get an ultrasound and biopsy when the mammogram was inconclusive. Her diagnosis was totally unexpected, he said, because she was young and healthy with no history of cancer in her family.

He told me Rachel had recently recovered from a mastectomy and how happy he was that she was doing so well. Throughout the story, I was struck by Russ' focus on his wife's strength and spirit. He wasn't embarrassed at all about a subject that most men might avoid – and certainly would not share with a stranger. No self-pity here, rather he had only admiration for his beloved wife whom he described as always so "full of life." He marveled at how she had taken her experience with breast cancer and turned it into a business, educating women about breast self-exams, what to do if you find a lump, and most important of all, how we must be our own advocates, and we shouldn't be afraid to question and even challenge decisions made about our health.

If Rachel had accepted her physician's advice to just watch her breast lump for a year, she may not have had such a hopeful outcome. "It can happen to anyone and early detection was the key," he said, and his wife was helping to get the word out to other women.

As he talked, his love and admiration for Rachel was radiating throughout the room. I was fighting back tears as he spoke. Not just tears of sympathy for this young woman who had endured such a horrible ordeal, but tears of respect and admiration for this man who clearly loved his wife more than life itself.

The tears also triggered a painful knowledge in my own heart, a knowing that my only purpose for existing, in **my** husband's opinion, was to make money – for him to spend, no matter the cost to me. Watching this devoted man describe his wife, using words like "courage," "respect," and "spirit," it was evident that she was, in his eyes, heroic, and that they were a very special couple. I immediately found myself asking if I could meet his wife and arrange for her to do a presentation at the company.

Rachel Hall: I was certain I was one of the luckiest women on earth. I had a great career, a wonderful, loving husband, a beautiful home, and loving family and friends surrounding me. My life was humming along so wonderfully, I never imagined what was lurking just around the corner that would bring my happy life to a screeching halt and turn my world upside down.

While lying in bed, I was haphazardly performing a breast exam. Much to my surprise, I found a small lump. I immediately thought, "I'm sure this is nothing. I'm young and healthy and there isn't any history of breast cancer in my family. I don't have any reason to be alarmed." I decided to call my doctor anyway.

The doctor I saw agreed there was a small lump, but because I was only 36 with none of the risk factors, his response was, "Let's just watch it for awhile." He didn't even order a mammogram.

At first I was relieved. He had told me just what I wanted to hear. I requested a mammogram anyway, because I thought I should at least get a baseline. After taking some routine views, they called me back for more. As before, the additional mammograms and ultrasounds were inconclusive. Again, the recommendation was to "watch it for awhile."

But my natural curiosity got the better of me. I wanted them to tell me exactly what this was, even though I was sure it wasn't cancer. I asked for a needle biopsy and saw a breast surgeon who suggested a lumpectomy instead, to avoid missing any malignant cells. I agreed.

The procedure was on a Friday; I took the day off work. I was back at work by Monday feeling pretty good. Tuesday I got the call. The doctor said she hated telling me over the phone, but she knew that I wouldn't want to wait to hear this news. She told me I had breast cancer and they would have to go back in to take more tissue.

The shock involved with the diagnosis was overwhelming, but the decisions that I had to make were even more overwhelming. I took four weeks to educate myself and finally made a heart-wrenching decision to have a mastectomy, mostly because the traditional methods of diagnosis were unsuccessful in my case. I did not want to wonder what else might be in there. I wanted to **choose life** and go forward feeling happy and healthy. But choosing to mutilate my body when I did not even feel sick was very difficult.

Losing my breast and recovering from the emotional as well as physical trauma was something I hope no other woman has to experience. Unfortunately, it happens every day, all over the world. Breast cancer can literally happen to anyone, regardless of lifestyle, and I believe that early detection is really the only step we can take right now to maximize our chances of survival. I wanted to find a way to get the word out to women, *"Don't be afraid to do self breast-exams, be afraid NOT to!"* After all, it had just saved my life.

I felt an urgency to get out there and teach women how to be their own advocates. I wanted to find a way to impress upon women, *"Don't settle for a decision from your doctor if it doesn't feel right for you. Listen to your gut, be pushy until you get the answers you are seeking."*

Early in my recovery I ran across a quote by the Canadian hockey player, Wayne Gretzky, "You miss 100 percent of the shots you never take." I knew that I had to take my shot. I wanted to form some kind of business to serve as a vehicle for getting my message to women, but I didn't know how to begin. I had never owned a business before and didn't know how we could manage financially if I left my job to do it. But my wonderful husband said he would "live in a tent with me" if that's what it would take to get my business going. Luckily, my boss was very understanding and allowed me to work part-time while I started my new adventure. My parents and family were also supportive and had always taught me that I could learn whatever I want to learn and be whatever I want to be.

And so it began. I took the first step and transformed the stumbling block of breast cancer into a stepping stone by forming Hall HealthMax, LLC. That first step has led to a path with unexpected twists and turns, but each one of them well worth the journey.

Renita continues: After Rachel's husband left my office that evening, I sat quietly, looking out the window at the setting sun and wondered, "Is it possible I could ever be loved and admired like that?" Deep inside my heart I knew, if I were to be diagnosed with something like breast cancer, my husband would leave me as fast as he could pack and get out the door (unless it looked as if I might die and he would be able to collect the life insurance).

Then I knew, I had to summon the courage, like the courage this woman named Rachel Hall possessed, and take a look at my life, and **choose** to live. If it meant leaving my husband, losing my home, losing my good credit rating, it didn't matter. I simply wanted to live. I wanted to find happiness, even a fraction of what this couple had. Regardless of whether there was someone out there who could love me the way Russ loved Rachel, I wanted to take the first step in loving myself and see where that might take me.

Just as Rachel had made the decision to choose life when she first felt a lump in her breast, I too chose to rid my life of any type of malignancy. As I watched the setting sun, the tears flowed freely down my cheeks and a calm passed over me for the first time in many years. I had taken the first step toward **LIFE** and it felt more right than anything had ever felt.

Rachel accepted my offer to speak about her experience to our employees. She was taking the first steps in building a pathway toward educating women about breast cancer, teaching them to be their own advocates, and impressing upon them the importance of early detection and how it can save our lives.

Yet as I've come to know Rachel personally, she has another message to everyone: "I am wonderfully happy, but some people aren't. I want to remind them that you only get one life. Don't wait for a near-fatal incident before you choose to live and choose to be happy . . . really happy. Take a look at your lives and summon the courage to make whatever changes you must in order to live **your** best life now. Take calculated risks. Build a support system for yourself and take the first step on your journey to a better life, a **happy** life."

Rachel didn't realize that in laying her first stepping stone with the Hall HealthMax presentations, it would soon lead her to her life's purpose. On my recommendation, a local newspaper published an article about her company. The result: Rachel was contacted by an international research company that was about to begin testing a new device for the early detection of breast cancer.

After a year of volunteer work with TCI Medical™, she began part-time employment, leading to her ultimately becoming the Director of Clinical Research. Now she manages clinical trials worldwide for the Centillion™ device, which does not require any radiation or compression. It is a digital imaging system that uses small, harmless pulses of electricity to detect cancer by measuring the conductivity readings in the tissue.

She is helping to create an innovative pathway for the early detection of breast cancer and providing hope to women across the world, as well as hope for future generations of women, and their loved ones, whose lives have been touched by cancer.

When I asked Rachel, "From the moment you were diagnosed with cancer, to this newfound career in medical research, what has been your greatest challenge?"

"Patience," she replied. "After you get a glance at death, you become very anxious to live."

As for me? I've been divorced nearly two years now. I'm financially stable (working one job), living alone (and loving it), and best of all, I'm living. I mean really **living**. I chase butterflies with my camera, I spend time laughing with newfound friends, I start my mornings with song and dance (literally!), and I keep company with a gentle-spirited man who cries when he hears the song, You Can't Hide Beautiful because he says it makes him think of me. I followed Rachel's advice and made a conscious decision to choose life and happiness, and I'm so very glad I did.

Stepping stones to happiness

- Choose to live your best life.
- Choose to be happy, really happy.
- Take control of your health, be your own advocate.

- Try some form of stress relief every day (deep breathing, yoga, exercise, reading, or even just smiling for five minutes straight).
- Never underestimate your ability to learn and transfer your skills.
- Make a list of the skills you have and the skills you want to learn. Take steps to tackle those new skills and keep updating your list.
- Build support groups and learn to network – join a church or a club (**www.nafe.com, www.workingmother.com, www.toastmasters.org**).
- Ask your employer about options like part-time work, job sharing, flexible schedules, or reinventing your job.
- Look to companies like BeautiControl, Mary Kay, and Avon if you need a step toward financial independence with built-in support groups.
- If you are in an unhealthy situation, whether it's a job, a marriage, or a friendship, take the first step to make changes or walk away.
- Remember that your thoughts are a sneak-preview of your life – create the life you want in your thoughts and they will become your reality.
- Practice being optimistic – surround yourself with optimistic friends and look for the value in every situation.
- Listen to your gut. Your intuition will tell you what is right for you.
- Don't try to be everything to everybody. Make changes to live your best life, and those who love you will admire that and follow suit (including your children).
- If you suspect that you are depressed, accept it as a chemical imbalance (not a character flaw) and ask your doctor for help. Life is too short to waste time feeling bad.
- Count your blessings – every evening write down a blessing that applies to something that day . . . even on the bad days.
- Purposefully think about what dreams you want to fulfill – write them down and read them often. Take steps to fulfill them.
- Remember, as Wayne Gretzky said "You miss 100 percent of the shots you never take." So take a shot!

Seeking Your Path:
Cultivating Potential from the Inside Out

Cindy Snow, RN, BSN, MPH, CHES

Cindy Snow is a registered nurse with a master's degree in public health and is a certified Life Coach. She began her nursing career in intensive care but soon realized that her true passion was helping people to proactively maintain their health. Since then Cindy has worked as an occupational health nurse for a large white-collar corporation providing one-on-one care to employees. After receiving her master's degree in public health, she broadened her reach in promoting a healthy lifestyle by working for a corporate health promotion department that used all types of media and marketing resources. Currently, Cindy is integrating her wellness talents to provide Life Coaching to individuals and groups, facilitating Nia Technique classes, and offering various other mind-body wellness and health promoting workshops.

Cindy Snow, RN, BSN, MPH, CHES
Cindy Snow, LLC
PO Box 119
East Berlin, CT 06023-0119
(860) 347-6484
CindySnow@erols.com

My Story

I had just completed my master's degree in public health and landed a terrific job with a large corporation. My career seemed ready to soar. I owned a beautiful home overlooking a brook and magnificent woodlands. I was active – mountain biking, hiking, skiing, any outdoor activity I wanted. I had many friends and family whom I saw often. I had a great garden and was a member of a local garden club. I was always busy, rarely sitting still for more than a moment. I felt I was on the superhighway of life.

Then, within one month of beginning this new job, my perspectives on my life and my health beliefs were positively challenged and significantly broadened. It happened innocently enough. At 9 a.m. I was offered this new job and then at 11 a.m. that same day I was asked if I wanted to go to the National Wellness Conference. No one in the company had attended before and "did I want to go?" Participants stayed in college dorms and ate dining hall food.

Immediately I said yes, why not. I'm always open to adventures. What I didn't realize was that what I would experience and learn at this conference would challenge my world like I'd never experienced before. At the conference I learned that what I had been taught was only one truth on health and healing throughout my nursing and graduate studies. Although the ideas I heard about body, mind, spirit, and emotional self were new to me, they resonated. Little did I realize that I would begin to learn about me along the way too and about making new choices.

Was this a quick and easy transformation? Absolutely not, but my initial excitement and inspiration from this conference fueled my fire to continue to explore and learn about what I had sampled. So in a remote Wisconsin college town, I met many people living, believing in, and implementing a variety of perspectives and methods on health in a wide array of settings. While there I also experienced a Nia Technique class at 6 a.m. one sticky summer morning. During this class I experienced utter joy moving, dancing in my body. I had believed I was not a dancer but Nia helped me change this notion. I was hooked.

So began my learning about a new way of helping people, one that embraced all aspects of a person with love and compassion. Each year I would return to the conference and explore and soak up new ideas. Two years after experiencing the Nia Technique for the first time, I took the training to be able to teach Nia because there were no teachers in my area. This holistic cardiovascular movement form was as much a learning experience about the Nia principles as it was about me.

I began to realize how disconnected I was with myself. I was numb and had shut down parts of myself. Again I returned to my life with excitement, yet now I was beginning to experience more and more dissonance. I wanted to be able to bring my body-mind-spirit concepts into my work but was unsure how. I was the one whose beliefs had changed, and I had difficulty explaining these concepts and ideas to others and thus doubted myself.

Again, another chance occurrence transpired just months later. I needed to take a vacation and had heard about the Hoffman Process at a previous workshop. A week-long retreat in May near the Berkshires didn't sound too bad. I knew it was a personal growth program, but I had absolutely no clue as to how deep and transformational it would be. And I thought this was going to be a vacation. The process helped me get in touch with myself and helped me to explore my inner passion and witness, with compassion, where I had been and who I had become and now where I wanted to go.

I didn't have any epiphanies but, adding this experience to the Wellness conference, I realized I was not living the life I desired. I wanted work in which I could fully embrace a holistic health perspective, so I sought Life Coaching training to add to my skill set. I realized I didn't want to continue to hide from life behind the walls I had created. I had allowed past heartache to shut out other possible relationships. I had believed myself to be open-minded, yet I became aware that I had allowed the influences of the fast-paced world, where opportunities abound and more is characterized as better, to sweep me up. I'd let the ideals of others guide my life and work, without checking in with myself. I realized I believed that my life was either laid out before me in a predetermined fashion or was pressed upon me by circumstances, and I was just to carry on. I'd forgotten about "me" and I'd forgotten who I was. I'd forgotten that life is truly a series of choices, and it was within my power and was my responsibility to make my choices.

I see now my path has been right in front of me. It's been a bumpy and uncertain road, but I wouldn't exchange a single moment of it. The bumps and snarls were the learning and experiences that made my growth richer. It has strengthened me. It's shown me my willpower and the support my lively spirit provides me. I've had to make some difficult choices, which haven't always been easy or clear. The perfect life I thought I had wasn't so perfect after all, but I now have the awareness to make different choices that matter to me.

Three years after attending the conference I've leaped into re-creating my life. It hasn't always been easy and I've had many people question my actions. But for the first time in my life I can honestly say that I'm living my authentic life. Right now I'm teaching Nia classes and providing Life Coaching to individuals and groups, yet I know there will be so much more. Opportunities that I could never have imagined are occurring. The beauty of cultivating potential from the inside out allows you to experience stumbling blocks as stepping stones instead of obstacles to the life you desire. Play with your perspectives, look for possibilities, and see if you can't see some different options.

Seeking Your Path:
Cultivating Potential from the Inside Out

Within each one of us is great potential and wonderful "good" to be shared with the world. The question is, are you willing to take the humbling journey? Like the beautiful rolling hillside, life can include a wide variety of experiences and textures. Sometimes it's easy, sometimes it's hard, it can be exhilarating, comical, and terrifying and sometimes all these emotions wrapped in the same moment. It's all part of the journey; it's all part of the plan.

For me taking the leap of faith to venture out on my own was scary and uncertain, but through listening to the whispers inside me and consciously planning, my life now feels so much more grounded and nurturing. This adventure, as I like to refer to it, has provided me with opportunities that I might not have seen or explored as well as allowed me to experience so much more love and joy in my life.

So how did I do it? What steps did I take? What path did I follow? How did I know what choices to make?

What I have to offer are ideas that worked for me. Pick and choose what might suit you and leave the rest. We all have different facets in our lives so no one method will work for everyone. Your life is rich with experiences and stepping stones. Listen to your heart and take what will nourish you and enjoy the ride!

Awaken to your life

Often I feel we truly know what we need to do, but it doesn't seem right, we're too busy, it seems ludicrous, or sometimes it goes against conventional wisdom. Don't discount these feelings. Allow them to percolate and surface. Listen to what your inner wisdom has to offer. Slow down and take some time to just pause. Don't be lured by media hype or infomercials. The solution you've been looking for, the answer, can only be found within you. Only you know what brings you true joy and happiness. The external world's job is to provide you with the array of choices. Your path is to pick the ones that are right for you.

Here are some ideas to help you listen to your inner wisdom:

- **Try journaling for 10 minutes a day** to get a snapshot of what's going on in your life. Empty your mind of the thoughts, sagas, and stories that may swirl in your head. Patterns and themes often present themselves when you start peeking at the chatter in your mind. Forget any rules about writing – just write. It's amazing what you learn.

- **Find a quiet spot** to walk or sit by your self. Take a conscious pause in life. Witness with nonjudgment the thoughts that bubble up, label them to become aware of their themes, and then allow the thoughts to flutter away. Just be. Taking time out of your day to be by yourself for even 10 minutes a day can be very enlightening. What do you hear, what do you sense, what do you feel during these quiet times?

Explore 'soul' ful cuisine

Confused, uncertain, overwhelmed as to what you want and where to go with your life? Mix a little curiosity with a little creativity and you are bound to find some tasty ideas. Sometimes we can get caught in the ruts or currents of life and the next thing you realize, I'm not where I want to be. How on earth did I get here?

Don't despair. Go back home. Grab your compass, otherwise known as the zip, the zest, your playful spirit, yes, a bit of the child within you. Explore your heart's desires. Here's an idea to help you tap into your creative spirit:

- **Create a collage.** Get a large piece of paper, some crayons, pens, scissors, old magazines, and go to town creating a map to your heart. With a collection of pictures, words, symbols, or drawings illustrate what nurtures you, what you value, what you want in your life, where you want to be, what your physical environment is like, what you enjoy doing. Set the timer for 30 minutes and you'll be amazed at what you create.

The balance of life

Personal and unique to each individual, we all have our own vision of what it means to live a balanced life. Sometimes due to certain circumstances, life feels lopsided and out of balance but then it springs back into place. Poof. Other times it feels out of order, and we may feel weighted down by one area of our life or another. The choices and decisions we make create the weight of different aspects in our lives. The balancing act is just a simple series of choices, though some of these "simple choices" may not seem so simple to choose. Balance is a process and not an item you can purchase at the store. It's the choices or non-choices you make that shape your world, your life. Want to peek at the balance in your life today?

- **How balanced is your world?** Each section of this diagram represents a piece of your life. This circle may include all the different aspects of your life, or you may need to add additional sections. Customize the circle to your life and then rate your current level of satisfaction in each section by drawing a line across each section. The center of the circle represents 0 and the outer rim represents 10, with 10 being fulfilled / satisfied. Connect the lines of the sections and check out how "round" the circle of your life appears today. What might a more fluid life look like to you?

The Circle of My Life

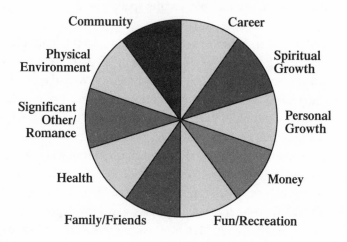

Simplify

Clearing the clutter, in a world where more is presumed to be better and super-sizing is everywhere, can seem overwhelming. By clearing space in your life and in your surroundings, you can have more freedom and areas to stretch toward your heart's desire. Clearing out creates space for new options or choices to come into your life. When you walk into your house or bedroom, how does it feel when you look around? How much of your day is spent worrying or taking care of "shoulds" and "tolerations"?

By clearing clutter from your environment and daily life, you step closer toward being clear of what you truly want in your life. Want to begin cleaning out?

- **Clean sweep a space in your house.** Start small. Take one closet or one room and sweep the space free of items and objects you no longer use or need. Your goal is to create empty space. For some this can be a difficult task because possessions often hold memories or emotions both positive and negative. Be clear with yourself. If you are not sure you are ready to part with a few items, take them out and place them in a storage box for one week before making your final decision. Notice how the space feels to you after completing the sweep. What do you notice? What do you sense? What does the energy feel like in this space now?

- **Clean sweep a day in your life.** Again, start small. Pick a day and take inventory of all the "shoulds" and "tolerations" that fill the day. Make a list. How much of your day is spent, as the great comedian and motivational speaker Loretta LaRoche says "shoulding' on yourself." I should be doing this, I should be going there, I should have gotten this and on and on. And how about tolerations? How much of your day is spent putting up with things? By taking stock of the "shoulds" and "tolerations" in your life you begin to see how much of someone else's life your life encompasses and how much of your life you're really living. Try eliminating one of these "shoulds" or "tolerations." Notice your energy level, how does it feel now?

Love and compassion

Life is a journey. We can be fearful tourists, sticking to the
well-worn paths in the hope that the ride will be smooth.
Or we can dare to sail uncharted waters.
– Author unknown

If you dare to be this type of life traveler, love and compassion for yourself are two ingredients that can sustain you along the way. This path is not always easy, but it is rewarding. Often fear of the unknown, the future, success or fear in general is what holds us back from our dreams and our heart's desires. Don't underestimate the power that love and compassion for yourself can have in your life. By first filling your well daily with self-love and self-compassion and then love and compassion for others, amazing opportunities will abound.

- **Send yourself love and compassion.** The next time something doesn't go as planned, instead of judging, comparing or berating yourself, send yourself love and compassion. Say a prayer or let the incident roll away. Don't hold on, let it go. Take a step toward your next stepping stone of possibilities.

Are you ready for a Life Coach?

The field of coaching is growing daily with more and more stories emerging of people achieving their dreams, goals, or balance they desire in their life. Having a Life Coach is a lot like having a personal trainer for your life, but the caveat is that you are at the steering wheel navigating. Life Coaching is for people ready to take action in their life. It involves an ongoing series of weekly conversations, typically a three-month commitment, where initially you reflect within yourself to get your bearings on your current life situation and then begin thinking and taking steps toward your dreams or goals. These 40-minute conversations elicit clear, inwardly directed thinking and decision making that leads you to your next steps.

Coaching is about discovering your options, clarifying your vision, and creating a strategy to have the life you desire. It's having someone always on your side, supporting and celebrating your successes. It's having someone keeping you focused on your agenda while helping you build awareness of what works for you and what doesn't. It's also having someone keeping you accountable to yourself while encouraging you to believe in all that you are capable of being. Your motivation is driven by you, your dreams and your desires.

The Life Coach is not there to tell you what to do. The coach is there to listen to what you say, what you don't say, and what you might have said between the lines. A coach will ask you the tough questions to make sure you've explored all your options and alternatives and that you are clear with what you want to do.

For some, hiring a Life Coach may be or seem out of financial reach. In this case, tap into the wisdom of a spiritual leader, respected friend, perhaps a mentor. Not all but most friends and family might be challenged to ask you the tough questions or be unable to see the other possibilities because of their emotional connections and investments they might have in your decisions or actions. Choose wisely.

Some coaches offer reduced fees for special situations. There are also coaches now connecting with nonprofit agencies to provide free coaching on a limited basis. Check out some community resources or the Web. Most coaches offer free sample sessions, and I recommend that you talk to and sample several before you begin. It only costs you a phone call if they're long distance. Ask about their coaching training and the philosophy of their program. Testing the waters allows you to assess the chemistry and compatibility of a potential coach before you dig in. As people seek coaches for all types of reasons, there are just as many types of coaches with varied backgrounds. Sample several to find one who will work for you.

Much of coaching today is conducted over the phone, which may be a new concept for you. It's one worth trying though. By interacting over the phone, from a quiet and distraction-free environment, you are able to focus with laser-light precision on yourself, on your thoughts, on your ideas, your dreams and goals. It's a conscious means of funneling your attention inward and facilitating awareness into your essence.

Most of all, Life Coaching works from a place of positive and believing that you're already whole. It's about highlighting your strengths instead of building up your limitations. It's about working with your unique gifts and talents and not trying to fit into any external standards. It's about being all that you can be and living the life of your dreams and your desires. It's about going for that joy-filled life you've dreamed about.

The 10 Health Commandments:
How to Make Choices that Lead to Health

Vicki Rackner, MD, FACS

Vicki Rackner, MD, is a board-certified surgeon and clinical instructor at the University of Washington School of Medicine. She has evaluated and treated surgical patients for over 10 years, conducted clinical research, taught medical students, testified as an expert in medical malpractice lawsuits, and served in leadership positions in her professional community. She is the Medical Editor of *The Hope Health Letter,* published by Seattle's Hope Heart Institute (www.HopeHealth.com).

Five years ago Vicki became a mother. After trying to do all and be all for the first six months of her son's life, she closed her private practice so that she could dedicate herself to parenting. Now that her son is in school, she has entered the next phase of her life – integrating the lessons learned from her experiences as a woman, a patient, and a healer. She has created a new kind of medical service that helps patients make informed health care decisions. She does not assume a patient's care; rather, she listens, translates medical information into understandable language, and helps guide her clients to the answer that is within.

If you have never heard of such a service, neither had she. She's making it up as she goes along, just as a mother does.

Vicki Rackner, MD, FACS
Medical Bridges
(425) 451-3777
rackner@medicalbridges.com
www.medicalbridges.com

My Story

I am a surgeon, and I have spent my career waging war on disease. I have come to see health as a path rather than a destination. It's a way of being in the world that involves your mind and body and heart and spirit, because they're all connected. Every decision you make can lead you in the direction of health – or toward illness.

As a surgeon, I can take you to the operating room and stop internal bleeding if you were in a car accident or remove the cancer in your breast or take out your gallbladder. To get here I have invested four years in college, four years in medical school, and five years as an apprentice in surgical residency. I have diagnosed and treated surgical patients for over 10 years, conducted clinical research, taught medical students, testified as an expert in medical malpractice lawsuits, and served in leadership positions in professional organizations.

**Despite this training and experience, I know
very little about how to keep you healthy.**

Here are some things I never learned in medical school and neither did your doctor:

Most disease doesn't have to happen: 75 percent of the diseases we currently treat are potentially preventable with lifestyle modification; 60 percent of cancer deaths could be avoided; 30 percent with smoking cessation and equal numbers with better dietary choices. Of the $1.4 trillion health care budget, 70 percent is spent on treatment of chronic disease. The government spends $1,390/person/year to treat disease and just $1.21/person/year to prevent it.

So why does your doctor focus on treatment of illness instead of preventing it? There are many reasons, including the economic forces that shape the practice of medicine. In addition, the survival of our species (or fear of extinction) has depended on the early detection of danger served by our brain's wiring to register fear more sensitively than any other emotion.

Five years ago I made the toughest choice in my life. At the time I was a surgeon with a thriving private practice. Most of my patients saw me for breast concerns. I felt blessed to be trusted and present in what often turned out to be a life-affirming journey into breast cancer. Then my son popped into my life at age 40. I did something I would never have imagined: I closed my practice to stay home with my child.

There are always so many layers to choices. The choice that I made was to make motherhood my priority for this period in my life. As the operating room door closed, another opened. I can't tell you that everyone lived happily ever after because we're just at "once upon a time."

The 10 Health Commandments:
How to Make Choices that Lead to Health

Our moral choices are guided by the 10 Commandments. I would like to offer you 10 health commandments that you can use to make choices that lead to health. Please don't get me wrong; even though I'm a surgeon I don't see myself as God. It's just that I open my eyes and see evidence that there are core Truths.

Health promotion is a way of seeing what's right. It's a way of saying "yes" to our bodies' own innate healing capacity. Our bodies are drawn to healing just as water runs downhill.

1. Begin your health journey from where you are.

You are on a path to health. There is no finish line, but the beginning is always where you are right now. When considering where you are now, your focus may shift to the past or the future. You might have shame or regret about choices that you have made in the past. The life you want can seem miles away. Mister Rogers' great gift was his ability to accept children as they are and for whom they are; he would want you to treat yourself in the same way.

A mother and her daughter visited an extraordinary field alive with the color of thousands of blossoming bulbs. The mother who loves gardening thought about how she could never do something as monumental as this. Then the property owner, now an old woman, came by. The visitors complimented her on the spectacular gardening achievement. The old woman reflected that every year she planted a handful of bulbs, and this garden is the result of a lifetime of modest efforts.

You are on a path to health. Each small step brings you closer. You might be arriving, but even the healthiest person hasn't arrived.

2. Manage your stress.

It's estimated that between 60 and 90 percent of doctor visits are to treat symptoms that are stress-related. It is not the stress itself, but rather your body's response to stress that affects health.

Here are some of my favorite stress-management tools:

Laugh. Ask at the family meal, "What happened today that made you laugh?" Or you can ask the question as part of the bedtime ritual.

Smile. The "facial feedback theory" is an idea that your facial expression will generate feelings, and a smile generates good feelings.

Supportive self-talk. Your daily 60,000 thoughts generally serve to keep you safe. You can replace these fear-based negative messages with supportive ones that you repeat – often.

Give up perfectionism. Did your mother tell you to leave the house with clean underwear in case you got in an accident? I have treated scores of trauma patients and never once heard a nurse or doctor comment on the condition of a patient's underwear.

3. Make a commitment to self-care.

You may just barely juggle work and children and getting everyone dressed in clean clothes each morning and having dog food in the house. For many the task that goes to the bottom of the list is the daily walk or the moment of solitude with a cup of tea or the lecture you so wanted to hear.

Yet health begins with self-care. It's almost a cliché, but when you're on an airplane you're instructed to put the oxygen mask on yourself before you put it on your children. Put your self-care on first, at the top of your to-do list. Go out for that walk. Take time to write in your journal. Make a commitment that self-care comes first. Always.

4. Support health with truth.

Political scientist Leo Rosten said, "We see things as we are, not as they are." You know that it feels good to tell the truth, even if it's hard – even if it means telling your partner about your eating disorder or sharing a cancer diagnosis with your children.

One form of managing a problem is ignoring it and hoping it will go away. Many people, when faced with health problems, do just that. So what's a little abdominal bloating, joint pain, or a headache? No big deal. But other problems should not be ignored: a breast lump, a change in a mole, blood in the stool. It's scary to think about what these symptoms may mean. But as my grandmother would say, "Dig into your bag of courage and face things, even if it's unpleasant or frightening."

So if you're faced with a choice, the path to health is always founded in honesty.

5. Consider new ideas with open skepticism.

The body is amazing. Last year I ran over a garden hose with the lawn mower. I spent over an hour trying to splice it back together. As I was driving to the hardware store to buy a new hose, I thought about the difference between the hose and blood vessels. When I sew arteries together in the operating room, they form a water-tight seal, right away. Medical scientists have identified cascades of biochemical events that occur during wound healing, but none speaks to the wonder of difference between arteries and hoses.

The placebo effect is another mystery. When doctors study new medications, they find that up to 40 percent of patients who get a sugar pill or placebo will get the same measurable responses as people who get the active ingredient, such as a reduction in blood pressure or heart rate.

Healing is mysterious. Let's be open to new ideas, no matter how outrageous. The major scientific "earth is round" breakthroughs are those that debunk commonly held beliefs. Let's acknowledge that today's leading-edge treatments may look tomorrow like the leeches of a primitive medical era – except that leeches are back and used in the treatment of surgically re-implanted fingers. Let's also hold all healing treatments, be it a new operation or a new cancer drug or an herb or energy healing, to the same scientific standards of proof.

6. Embrace health promotion.

My dentist is in his 60s. When he started his practice, he spent over half his time making and fitting dentures. He says it's reasonable to think that a child born in this decade may never have a single cavity. This is an example of the power of health promotion.

Our mothers and grandmothers wrote the book on health promotion. They told us: Eat your fruits and vegetables. Get a good night's sleep. Exercise. Don't smoke.

Here are a few more:

Breathe. Breathing is the core of most meditative practices. Anytime you're stuck in traffic is a chance to focus on breathing.

Develop a spiritual connection. Be connected to something greater than just yourself.

Give. Think of how you felt the last time you gave of yourself especially if the giving was unscripted.

Stay curious. Learn something new every day.

Know what's important. If you've had the great fortune of being with someone who is dying, you know that at the end what counts most is how much love you've given and gotten.

Learn to say no. Say no to things that clutter your time or your home or your energy.

7. Give your intuition a voice.

There is a voice inside you that knows what's happening in your body. I would ask my patients referred for breast concerns whether they thought they had a serious problem. In almost 100 percent of the cases patients accurately predicted whether or not they had breast cancer.

I have examined the breasts of thousands of women, but I will never know your breasts as well as you do. They're your breasts, and you know if the lumpiness is different in some way that I can't remember since your last exam or recorded in your medical file. You have another advantage over me. I do my examination with the nerve endings in my examining fingers; you also have nerve endings in your breasts. Your hunches about your health are like your nerve endings that no doctor, no matter how skilled, has.

You will also have an intuition about whether you and your doctor are a good fit. The foundation of a doctor-patient relationship is trust. It's important that you can trust the physician to do what's needed for that job, and you might want different things from different doctors. Communication skills may be a top requirement for your primary care doctor, and technical skills are vitally important in your surgeon. A doctor who is the right one for even your best friend might not be the right one for you.

Your intuition will also guide you to the medical choice for treatment that works best for you in a given situation. It's just a matter of taking time to listen.

8. Recognize that doctors are people.

You would like to believe that you will get perfect care from an all-knowing doctor that will guarantee cure. I wish it were so. Let's look behind the curtain of that all-powerful Dr. Oz:

Doctors make mistakes. Up to 100,000 patients died in the hospital in 1999 as a result of preventable medical errors. That's more patients than died from AIDS or car accidents or breast cancer in the same period. Mistakes happen because the system is complex, and care is delivered by people and people make mistakes.

Doctors don't know everything. Technology and the Internet are advancing medical knowledge and making it accessible at an amazing rate. It is impossible for your doctor to be the expert on large numbers of medical conditions. You may find that you know more about your illness than your doctor does.

Doctors don't have magic wands. No miracle cure produces the perfect outcomes without risk. Any treatment, be it a medication or an herbal remedy or an operation, has risks with no guarantee of cure.

Doctors will most likely not suggest and support health promotion strategies. Right now there's no glory in health promotion. The glory is captured in an ER episode in which the surgeon cracks the patient's chest in a heroic life-saving intervention. It would get better ratings than the new show Doctor's Office that shows a doctor congratulating the patient on the success of controlling his diabetes with diet and exercise or her ability to quit smoking.

Doctors have little proof that treatments work. Most of the treatments that doctors give are offered because that's the way it's been done. There is an evolving field of evidence-based medicine that subjects treatment to clinical testing.

Doctors have feelings. Doctors get angry, sad, and frustrated just like you do. I want my patients to do well, and I experience profound sadness when patients have complications or die. Surgeons have a weekly meeting called morbidity and mortality (or M&M) in which all the surgeons learn the lessons taught by patients who have had bad outcomes. This is not a mechanism for doctors to express feelings. Efforts at denying the feelings are usually unsuccessful and may explain the high incidence of alcoholism and grumpiness among physicians.

9. Honor your own healing style.

Each of you responds to the stress of illness in a different way. Some want all of the information that is available. Others don't even want to know about the possible side effects of medication because they feel that they are suggestible. Some want to make all their own decisions; others want to rely on the recommendation of the doctors they trust. We're in a time of profound change in the very nature of the doctor-patient relationship. It is evolving from a relationship that looked like a parent-child relationship to an adult-adult relationship. Do what works best for you.

10. Actively participate in your health care.

The single best strategy to getting health care that is safe and effective is your active participation. This does not mean that you will become your own physician. Even physicians know better than to diagnose and treat themselves. This does not mean that you will be asked to make all of your medical choices alone; you want the experience and support of a trusted physician to help you make the tough choices. Your goal is to get quality health care.

If you leave your appointment with unanswered questions, you are in good company. Even high-functioning professionals face challenges in applying their skills in the doctor's office. I invite you to think about your level of satisfaction with your doctor and identify barriers you might have that keep you from asking for what you want.

For some it's as easy as just finding the right words and the courage – and sometimes practice to use them.

- If you see three specialists and feel as if no one's in charge, you can say to the most likely doctor candidate, "I like the idea of team medicine. Will you be my quarterback?"
- Or when the nurse is taking your blood pressure in the exam room while you sit in a paper gown, "I already feel so naked. Is there a way of getting dressed after the doctor examines me and before we make a plan?"

- Or to the receptionist scheduling your appointment, "I am facing a decision that will affect the rest of my life, and I really want to understand my options. How can I schedule an appointment that's an hour long? I would be willing to pay out-of-pocket for time my insurance company does not cover."

———— ◆ ————

It's hard to be a patient. Our medical system is showing strain at every seam. Care is decentralized, and it's hard to find a doctor who can spend more than 20 minutes with you to integrate the advice you're getting from multiple doctors. The information on the Internet is both empowering and overwhelming. You don't know whether to go to your doctor or the health-food store for treatment of your most recent symptoms. You know that there are things you can do to stay healthy, but the recommendations seem to change every week. You're not sure that your doctor has all the information needed to make medical recommendations that are customized for you.

So how do you get good health care?

Your job as a patient is to make important medical choices, and these choices bring special challenges. These are often decisions that will affect the rest of your life. There are no right answers, only choices that are best for you at this time in your life. You're the best person to make this choice. To make matters worse, you may not be at your best if you are sick. Many patients simply feel abandoned by the health care system at a time they most need to be supported.

Over the years I've observed an increased number of phone calls that start out with, "Vicki, do you have a minute?" The phrase alerts me to put on my doctor hat to help the caller make tough choices at a stressful time. I have been so concerned by this trend that I have started a company I call Medical Bridges. It's intended to be the bridge between the care patients want and the care they're getting. I don't assume a patient's care; rather, I listen to the patient's story, help identify the issues, gather options, and help guide patients to the best choice. You have a knowing about what the best choice is. The task is finding the voice and listening.

Sometimes listening is the greatest gift you can give someone, and it's hard to come by. Listening takes time, and doctors, most of whom are employees, don't have control over their schedules. There is also therapeutic value in giving a voice to fear and diffusing it with understandable information. If you have the courage to say, "I'm afraid of dying under anesthesia," you have the chance to learn that the operating room is statistically one of the safest places to be – much safer, in fact, than the car trip to the hospital.

Our health care system is on the brink of collapse. I think we are on the verge of a different and better health system. I think it will incorporate health promotion, recognition of the power of the relationship between doctor and patient, and an acknowledgment of the connection of the mind, body, heart, and spirit.

So what is health? It's being who you are, well-tuned, fully engaged in the business of living in each moment. I wish you luck on your journey.

The Most Dangerous Question You Can Ask God

Kathy (Kate) Bailey

Billed as the "Queen of Health Fairs," Kathy Bailey started one of the nation's first corporate wellness companies in 1985 in California. People Growers of America has since assisted literally thousands of companies to organize on-site employee education programs aimed at improving the minds, bodies, and spirits of America's mighty workforce.

While studying educational psychology at San Diego State University, Kathy realized the same learning principles used in elementary education applied to adults as well. She discovered people learn best by involvement of all the senses and interaction with their environment. Kathy saw corporate expos – complete with healthy food samples, music, screenings and hands-on activities – as perfect venues for supporting positive lifestyle changes. Her company has now expanded throughout the West Coast and recently went nationwide with an online component, the NationalWellnessForum.com. This popular Web site features a complete directory of local exhibitors and providers – a

"Virtual Health Fair" for employees who can't access an on-site event – and is home to the National Association of Wellness Coordinators, an online networking organization of professionals responsible for group wellness education.

Kathy most enjoys teaching her popular workshop, *Trade Secrets of Corporate Marketing,* in which she shares her hard-won knowledge with humor and a special insight gleaned from 20 years in the industry. Though her speaking schedule requires extensive travel, Kathy makes her home in the Northwest, where she can be close to her daughters and grandchildren. Her younger daughter, Katrina Voshall, is studying for her college degree, and her older daughter, Windy Baty, is CEO of People Growers, Oregon Division.

Kathy Bailey, CEO
People Growers of America
(877) 742-7462
Kathy@peoplegrowers.com
www.NationalWellnessForum.com

My Story

I languished in the bathtub in the middle of the day, drinking what I call a lonely glass of wine . . . the one you drink when nothing works, and escape seems the best of all options.

At the tender age of 38 I had come to the end of my rope. I saw no future, none at all. How could I, star of my own splendid Broadway-quality life (especially if you count all the drama queen scenes) have come to the place where Lancer's and a lukewarm bubbleless bath were my just desserts? In my self-pitying state, "The Question" entered my head.

If you knew my whole life history up to that point, you probably would have told me "Shut-up, you whiny girl!" Yah, OK. I had a great childhood. Nice middle-class white child, raised on a farm in the lush California San Joaquin Valley by hardworking parents who made sure I had dance and piano lessons. My Miss American Pie life looked like this: drama classes, high school cheerleader, a scholarship to go around the world on Chapman College's University Afloat, wed to my high school sweetheart, two healthy daughters, a sad but friendly divorce 14 years later, no real-life traumas to speak of.

Five years after my first daughter was born, I graduated from San Diego State with honors, just two credits short of a teaching credential. I fell into a summer job working for Jack LaLanne Nutrition Centers, which flowered into a career. By age 28, I was winning gaudy trophies for record-breaking vitamin sales and loving every minute of the 15 minutes of fame Andy Warhol promised each of us.

Mini-sizing a long story, I went on to manage five nutrition centers and later moved into industrial medical marketing. For those readers who don't know what that is, don't worry, almost no one does. Basically, I visited large companies and urged them to send their sick and injured to the three hospital emergency rooms I represented. My work stations were in the ERs of medical centers, and I watched in dismay as a steady stream of patients arrived at our doors. Most of them had one thing in common: they were there because of the poor lifestyle choices they made.

I saw the tragic results of lives filled with drugs, alcohol, unhealthy diets, dangerous relationships, and inadequate prenatal care. It was then the seed of destiny was planted in my heart. I vowed to do something to support these precious souls to take better care of their bodies, minds, and spirits. But how?

In the male-dominated world of emergency room medicine, I quickly hit the glass ceiling, which my naturally Pollyanna rose-colored-glasses personality didn't even realize existed. Not noticing the ceiling for its transparency, I banged on it loudly and inelegantly enough to get myself fired, as my boss explained, for "trying to be the Chief when you are expected to be an Indian." This was a cause for dismissal I couldn't help but take as a backhanded compliment. Still, I had lost a good-paying job and was slammed with a blow to self-esteem some of us know too well.

Jobless, hopeless – I asked "The Question."

This brings us back to the little suburban bathroom in El Cajon, California, where no aromatherapy candles burned, no Yani tapes played. Just me, jobless at 38, gazing down hopelessly at what looked suspiciously like viral cellulite depositing itself on my thighs as I watched.

It was then that I asked the question no woman better ask, unless she has the ovaries to handle the answer.

"Oh, God what do you want me to do for You? What is my life's purpose in Your Plan?" Now since I've already fessed up to the wine thing, you might be a little skeptical of what I'm going to tell you happened next. But it did happen.

I heard a voice speak loudly behind me in my left ear: "Teach only Love, for that is what you are." Shades of Jerry Jampolsky!* What the heck did that mean?

"God," I said out loud and rather disrespectfully, "Do you mean I should be a minister or something? That's crazy! I don't even belong to an organized religion!"

Then, as if by explanation, across the bathroom wall was written, as clear as day, "People Growers of America."

Getting weirder and weirder, I thought. But, hey, I might as well ask. "What is People Growers, God?"

Then I was shown, holographically, the whole of People Growers as it exists today and even into the unfulfilled future. I had been given the complete blueprint for creating a company to teach America's work-force how to take better care of their bodily temples through good nutrition, exercise, and positive life management skills. People Growers would gather together local experts in these fields, convince them to fund this project, and "take it to the corporations" via on-site Health and Wellness Expos. What a great idea, God!

Not!

If I was in despair before this vision, I now flirted with the idea of sliding down in the bathtub until the tepid water covered my face forever.

Bargaining with God, or how to lose an argument and win your life

"Yoo-hoo, Big G," I needed to point out, "Perhaps you have me confused with someone who CAN!" I screamed! "Perhaps You, in Your

---

*Jerry Jampolsky is the well-known author of *Teach Only Love* (highly recommended reading).

Infinite Optimism, may have overlooked the fact that I am in a real shaky relationship with a handsome recovering alcoholic. Maybe you didn't notice I'm too old to start a new business! Excuuuuuusme, but I don't have a cent to my name, I own a house with a huge mortgage, I'm on disability 'cause that last job made me sick to my stomach, and I have two kids to raise without a day-to-day father figure. May I add that I haven't Clue One as to how to get this whole thing started, and I'm totally NOT NOT NOT going to do it!"

With that, I drank the last of the warm wine in the bottle and slunk to my bed like the loser I knew I was.

What happens when you ask God THE QUESTION, get a definite, holographic, psychedelic, audio, visual, direct answer, and you say, "NO"? Well, let me tell you, Sister, it ain't pretty. First, the bowels let loose, or at least they did in my case. Let's call is spiritual dysentery. Did I mention weakness, fatigue, and general confusion? I seemed beside myself, out of alignment, and getting worse by the day. I was miserable and felt cut off from my kids, my friends, and my Source. Like Jonah, I refused to go to Nineveh and ended up being semi-digested by a whale of a bad experience.

We Central Valley people know where to go to find our roots – into the Sierra Nevada Mountains, from whence our alluvial soil comes. So one Friday I hustled my boyfriend and five-year-old daughter Katy into the car and off we drove to "get back to nature" in my favorite soul-soothing place, Yosemite National Park.

The first night we had to camp outside the park because, of course, I was so out of the flow I couldn't even manifest a decent camp-ing spot. In the morning I woke with a raging migraine. It was so excruciating that when Katy began screeching for a bowl of cereal, I went after her neck with my hands ready to choke her to death. (This episode remains one of my daughters' favorite kidding-Mom stories to tell at family reunions.) Alarmed by my uncustomary display of mur-derous intent, my boyfriend rushed me into Yosemite and found us a camping spot on the Valley floor. Convinced that I was dying of a brain aneurysm or something worse, I begged him and Katy to go get the paramedics and get me off the hill and into Fresno, where I could die with the best possible medical attention.

There I lay alone, on the grass in a makeshift bed in the blinding sunlight, left to suffer and wonder how things could have gotten this far out of control. I squinted up and saw the sheer face of Half Dome towering above me, just another affirmation of my small, useless self. "Jesus, Jesus, Jesus," I whimpered. "Take me now. I just can't stand the pain." I really and truly gave in, and quit.

Just then, a hang glider appeared at the edge of Half Dome. Standing there like Apollo, wings spread wide and sure of his mission, he poised a full minute. I wondered what was going on in his head. Was he praying? Was he taking in the view? Was he scared? Could he see all of us campers far down below him, like so many Monet-inspired color splotches? Was he checking his gear? Then, breathtakingly, he simply put one foot forward and stepped off the rock cliff. He just took one big step, legs apart, wings soaring. He took his time coming down, caught the updrafts and spiraled lazily over the Valley floor. To me, he looked like an angel with the yellow sun above him and the birds darting around him.

Then the Creator, the One with the Word, don't you know, whispered to me, "If he can take that first step, that leap of faith, so can you my dear child, Sister Kate." Yes, I was called Sister. I heard those exact words whispered in my ear. It was a huge, huge moment.

The hang glider happened to land close to me. It was not Robert Redford, but an average Joe who was completely unaware of the lesson he had just given me, which was to change my life forever.

The paramedics arrived just then, sirens screaming, with Katy in the front seat, her face knotted with worry. I simply sat up, with a look of incongruous serenity on my face and announced that I was sorry, no need, headache was mysteriously gone. Feeling absolutely euphoric, I announced that we were renting bikes with virtually our last bit of cash and touring the Park. And by the way, on Monday I was opening the doors of People Growers of America. And so it was!

Saying "Yes" to God or taking the adventurous path

I have to admit I was as scared as if I were about to hang glide for the first time myself. But I knew I was not alone. I knew absolutely and positively that People Growers was what I was destined to accomplish. I felt like the Blues Brothers on a mission for God!

I started my search where any self-respecting consumer would. I grabbed the Yellow Pages and turned to "Chiropractors." From the age of 16 to 28 I had suffered from migraines regularly (that one in Yosemite was the first I'd had in 10 years). In 1973 I had been rear-ended by an extremely well-insured tow truck and, due to a series of serendipitous circumstances, found myself in a chiropractor's office being treated for a severe whiplash injury. He identified the cause of my headaches as a compression of the second and third cervical discs dating back to my cheerleading days. The first adjustment gave me incredible, immediate relief, and a subsequent series of treatments healed me completely. I vowed that I would introduce this miraculous science to others if I ever had the opportunity. The opportunity was now.

But who to call? My chiropractor had long ago retired. So I simply asked for Divine Guidance to help me on this one, ran my fingers down the columns, and picked one when my finger was led to stop. Five came up, all together. I took a deep breath, reached for the phone, and called each one. Whatever I said, I created enough curiosity to convince them to meet me for breakfast at a very nice restaurant. How I was going to pay for $8 breakfasts for each of them was beyond me, but by this time I was simply operating by faith. Logic had long ago shrugged and walked away.

The breakfast meeting found me with sweaty palms, dry mouth, and a rudimentary business plan created on an old Underwood. I didn't tell them the metaphysical aspects of the project. I simply told them I planned to start a health fair company. The first topic I wanted to include was chiropractic and the story of my own healing experience.

At the end of the presentation I asked each one for a $400-a-month contribution. I needed the first $400 immediately. Get this for a miracle: Each of them reached in their pockets, pulled out checkbooks, and within five minutes there in front of me lay $2,000, the exact amount of seed money I figured I needed. And one of the generous chiropractors graciously picked up the bill for breakfast.

Life offers the gift of purpose

I wish for each of you to feel the indescribable exhilaration and grateful humility I felt as I drove home that day. Just a month before I felt I had no reason to live. Now I had been given the greatest gift I believe life can offer to us, the opportunity to serve. The gift of purpose.

The miracles continued to happen. They still do! Doors swung open – doors I didn't even know existed. Supportive and talented staff, without whom I never could have survived, came from the most unlikely places. Dentists and medical groups called ME when they heard what I was doing. At my first health fair at Coca-Cola, we found an executive in the initial stages of a heart attack and rushed him to the hospital, perhaps saving his life. At the same fair we also found glaucoma symptoms in a young woman, who because of her age would have never thought to have the free test we administered.

The Universe confirmed to me then, and confirms to me now, that we are all stewards of each other's health and well-being. God called me "Sister" because that's who we truly are to each other. Where one person ends and another person begins is so nebulous as to be nonexistent. That is what I know. That is what I hope and pray each one of you continues to discover.

And whatever you do, ask "The Question." But just be prepared to say "Yes." Then take the courageous steps to make it all happen.

Because if you take care of God's business, God will take care of yours.

The Most Dangerous Question You Can Ask God

How rich are you?

As my story proves, you can start a business with almost no cash on hand. But the success of your business . . . indeed your life . . . depends on your Personal Power Bank Account. Perhaps you haven't quite figured out why certain days seem opulent and others seem desolate, independent of your financial situation. It's because we all consciously or unconsciously deposit or withdraw from this account daily.

Here are some strategies for building your personal power bank account and to help you get in touch with your only true and eternal life legacy. This is the currency you do take with you.

Personal Power Bank Account Withdrawals

These acts and attitudes are guaranteed to impoverish your spiritual and personal life:

Break your word to yourself and others:

- You avoid facing addictions and lie about them to yourself and others.
- You don't keep promises and commitments large and small.

Attach meaning to things that have no meaning:

- You often take offense, forcing someone else to defend his or her innocence.
- You withhold affection when feeling offended or rejected.

Be paralyzed by "analysis":

- You think, obsess, list pros and cons, or worry about "getting it right."
- You don't complete relationships.
- You don't handle regrets, forgiveness, and resentment involving parents, siblings, lovers, and friends. [Hint: They are "handled" when the other person says they are.]

Be run by emotions:

- You often wonder about reasons for your unpredictable actions and outbursts.
- You often feel remorse and shame.
- You suspect that anyone who seems to have a larger Personal Power Bank Account than yours is dangerous (paranoia).

Personal Power Bank Account Deposits

These acts and attitudes are guaranteed to enrich your spiritual and personal life:

- Own a clear vision of your life's mission and have a concise verbal statement of that mission and vision.
- Keep your word even in little things.

- Turn addictions into preferences, or let them go altogether (self-discipline).
- Acknowledge and sincerely compliment others frequently as soon as the thought enters your mind.
- Complete relationships – handle regrets, resentments, and forgiveness.
- Control emotions – be difficult to anger.
- Take "Ready, Fire, Aim" approach to life.
- Take affordable risks.
- "Fail forward" toward success. Appreciate the journey as well as the destination.
- Trust intuition and "gut feelings."
- Be "coachable" and eager to learn from others.
- Celebrate life – live in the moment.
- Be inspired by passion, dedication, and purpose.
- Discover your unique set of personal values and live by them.
- Place as high a value on others' lives as on your own.

These five powerful phrases are guaranteed to enrich your life:

- 5 Most Powerful Words: "You can count on me."
- 4 Most Powerful Words: "I need your help."
- 3 Most Powerful Words: "I appreciate you."
- 2 Most Powerful Words: "Thank you."
- 1 Most Powerful Word: "Yes!"

You Can Play: Your Lifelong Commitment to Taking Care of Your Self

Brenda Caryn Loube, MS

Brenda Loube's entire career has been in the field of health and fitness. Her passion is helping people improve their health, prevent disease and illness and improve the quality of life.

Brenda's diverse health and fitness background began at Towson State University, where she earned a BS in physical education in 1974. These credentials, coupled with a desire to teach, secured her the position of fitness instructor and supervisor for several organizations. During this time, she became involved with cardiac rehabilitation. Within a year, she received an academic scholarship to the University of Wisconsin-LaCrosse where she earned a MS in physical education with an emphasis in cardiac rehabilitation.

Georgetown University Hospital was Brenda's first site as a cardiac exercise technician, where she later became a cardiac rehabilitation and exercise specialist for the entire hospital. As such, she founded and implemented their in- and out-patient cardiac rehabilitation programs, while also teaching at Georgetown's School of Nursing. She was soon recognized as a principal resource for groups seeking an expert speaker on the subjects of both heart disease prevention and rehabilitation.

The field of rehabilitation seemed a natural springboard into the area of health promotion and preventative health programs. Brenda was recruited by Life Centers, Inc., in McLean, Virginia, to develop and administer health and fitness screenings for its entire membership. Within a year she was formulating programs for an increasingly wide variety of interests and needs in the commercial health club environment.

Her experience in health, fitness, recreation, and cardiac rehabilitation was pivotal in the formation of Corporate Fitness Works, Inc. (CFW), of which she is President and co-owner. CFW is a full-service fitness and health management organization serving the needs of businesses, government agencies, office park developers, hospitals and retirement communities throughout the United States. Brenda conducts coaching, leadership and team training, leads program development and implementation, new business development, and champions the public relations for the company.

Brenda's affiliations in professional organizations include Women Business Owners of Montgomery County Board Member, Maryland State Advisory Council on Physical Fitness Board Member, member of Wellness Councils of America and International Council on Active Aging, and member of the Advisory Board to Marymount University's Department of Health and Human Performance. In November 1993, she was inducted into the Greater Washington Jewish Sports Hall of Fame for achievements in racquetball and softball.

Brenda Loube has extensive experience in programming of wellness, fitness, recreation, special interest groups, and special events for all age groups including children, adults, older adults, and special needs individuals. Brenda's knowledge and enthusiasm for her work are eclipsed by her widely acknowledged ability to share her vitality with her clients.

Brenda Loube, MS, FAWHP
President, Corporate Fitness Works
18558 Office Park Drive
Montgomery Village, MD 20886
(301) 417-9697 ext. 13
bloube@corporatefitnessworks.com
www.corporatefitnessworks.com

My Story

It could have happened yesterday. I was 9. The fifth-grade boys were gathering on the Oakview School playground after class to play dodge ball. What fun, I thought, as I joined the lineup when the captains began choosing teammates. It got to the end of the selection, and there was no one left but me. I just stood there – all by myself.

At first no one said a word. It took all the strength and energy I had to ask, "Whose team am I on?" One boy fired back, "Can't you see, girls can't play."

I didn't know what to say. So I said nothing, although I wanted to crawl in a hole and cover myself up. I didn't know what to do with myself, so I picked up my books and began walking home. Tears poured down my face.

This wasn't fair. I knew I could play with the best of them. But it didn't matter if I was a good athlete. What mattered was that I was a girl. I was not a boy; therefore, I could not play.

Have you ever been told you could not do something, but in your heart you knew you could? I'll bet you were not even given a chance to show what you could do. No matter what your interest or ability to participate in sports, this is the experience many women have when it comes to being physically fit or active in recreational sports. We are taught that "exercise" is something we do for short periods of time in an effort to change our weight or fit into an outfit for a special event. What about having goals of finding our optimal fitness level or simply having a good time?

You deserve to play, just as I was determined to prove that I could play. I did not say anything to anyone at the time, not even to my parents or my brother. But I set my intention: I decided to work hard and practice developing my skills, whether it was in softball, basketball, or a project in business. I wanted so much to prove that I could play with the best of them.

Developing a passion for sports

With this goal in mind, I worked hard to hone my athletic ability. Fortunately, my brother, Jacky, who was six years older than I, always asked me to warm him up during his sports seasons. He played them all.

Brenda Loube

The one sport I can remember the most was softball. Jacky would take me out in the backyard to field grounders. The object of the game was to throw the softball on the ground trying to make the other person miss it. I would do everything I could to be the best at whatever I was doing. I worked hard to beat him not knowing why I wanted to be the best. He was always so much better than I was. The only way I could win would be if I could tie his feet together.

I kept practicing and Jacky helped me develop my athletic skills. He was an excellent role model and my mentor, as well as a great athlete. Thanks to his help, I played four varsity team sports in high school – volleyball, basketball, softball, and field hockey – played four years of varsity softball in college, and lettered in high school and college. At age 16, I tried out and played second base for a women's semi-professional fast pitch team that later came in second in the country.

One of my dreams was to be a professional athlete like so many women during my generation such as Chris Evert or Billy Jean King, but for whatever reason – lack of opportunities being a big one – I did not have the chance to see what it would have been like.

Having a passion for sports, I earned my undergraduate degree in physical education with the hope of teaching and fostering the love I had for sports and physical activity to my students. Because, there were no full-time teaching positions after graduation, I worked a number of part-time jobs. I substitute taught for a while and realized quickly that the curriculum needed to emphasize lifetime fitness and to teach children the fun of being healthy and fit through daily physical activity.

I also worked as a fitness specialist at the Jewish Community Center in the cardiac rehabilitation program. I had no prior training in cardiac rehabilitation, so I was fortunate to attend a training workshop at the University of Wisconsin-LaCrosse, which is where I received my master's degree in physical education with an emphasis in cardiac rehabilitation.

After graduation I began playing racquetball and won numerous state and regional titles, and eventually a national title for my age group. My first job after grad school was at Georgetown University Hospital. I started as a cardiac exercise technician administering diagnostic treadmill tests, and in just a short while I rewrote my job description and became the first cardiac rehabilitation specialist at the hospital. I then became the founder of Georgetown University Hospital's Cardiac

Rehabilitation Program and went on to teach the cardiac rehabilitation program at Georgetown University Nursing School. Soon I became the exercise specialist for the entire hospital.

My wellness journey begins

During that time I helped many patients begin their journey of wellness and daily physical activity. I believed that everyone could benefit from some form of physical activity in their daily routine regardless of their physical limitations or health condition. As long as the doctor would write a prescription for exercise, I introduced patients to my world – the world of exercise.

I wondered, what could I do to prevent heart disease? Especially after seeing so many heart attack victims and those stricken with disease, I wanted to approach exercise on the front end. My journey took me there. I worked a few years in the commercial health club setting and as a consultant for a fitness management firm.

In 1988, my business partner Sheila Drohan and I started our own company called Corporate Fitness Works. We continue to be the proud owners of a successful health promotion and fitness management firm based in Maryland. We currently have 29 centers across the country serving businesses, hospitals, office park developers, government agencies, residential and retirement communities.

My personal mission is to continue to grow in order to prevent unnecessary diseases and health conditions for all those we serve. We are helping our participants to realize how physical activity can be an integral part of their lives My hope for you is that you will bring "play" back into your life!

You Can Play: Your Lifelong Commitment to Taking Care of Your Self

How you can reach your health potential

Reaching our health potential is something I feel all of us deserve. But what does that mean? It means being physically healthy and in the state of health where you have the energy to do anything and everything you desire to do.

You have the ability to be as healthy as you can be and to reach your life goals with zest, positive energy, and stamina. My question for you is this: Do you want to reach your health potential? If your answer is yes, then I have the solution. The simple answer is daily physical activity. But here's the real question: What would it take for you to make daily physical activity a priority?

Physical activity has always been a priority in my life. I played sports as a young child and continued playing through high school and college. Today in midlife I walk, hike, cycle, lift weights, stretch daily, and compete in racquetball. Physical activity is a way of life for me not only personally but professionally. When I don't exercise, I really miss it and long for the next exercise opportunity. It might sound crazy, but I look forward to vacation so I can have endless amounts of time to enjoy moving my body, sweating, exerting myself, and subsequently really feeling good about myself. It is a great feeling and the reward is the energy you feel.

Over the past 29 years in the health field I have listened to numerous reasons not to exercise, for example: *there's no time, family commitments, too difficult, it hurts, it's uncomfortable, I don't like it, I can't do it, I'm self-conscious and afraid people are looking at me, too expensive, not motivated,* or *I'm too lazy.* Why do we tend to make these excuses?

No quick fixes

Most of us are looking for quick fixes, but truly there is no substitute for doing some form of physical activity every day. Our bodies were meant to move, to be active and mobile. Professional athletes train daily for hours to fine tune their physical bodies for the sole purpose of top performance in their sport and to win the game.

We can look at our bodies and overall health in the same way, but instead of training for sport, we train for life. The benefits we can achieve are so overwhelming that all of us should want to achieve this level of well being.

Some of the benefits of physical activity are preventive in the areas of high blood pressure, obesity, elevated cholesterol, heart disease, breast cancer, colon cancer, diabetes, arthritis, and osteoporosis. Other health benefits include weight control, reduction of stress, stronger muscles and joints, improved balance, and reduced symptoms of anxiety and depression. In fact, the chemicals our body produces when we play create a natural "high" – a surefire stress reducer.

A walk a day for optimal health

So what will it take for you to reach your health potential and get moving? Just moving can be so simple that anyone can accomplish it. We tend to make it harder than it really is. All I am referring to is five to 10 minutes a day, each day of the week. Five minutes of walking with comfortable walking shoes is the beginning. Eventually these five minutes get longer and longer as everything comes together: the value, the benefits, the time commitment, your attitude, and how you feel. In the end, I visualize for each of you 30 minutes of activity per day. You deserve it. You are entitled to feel the best you can feel. You owe it to yourself. It is up to you to care that much about yourself.

What do you need to get started? The most important piece of equipment is a pair of shoes that do not hurt after you wear them for a walk. Make sure you go to a store that understands how to fit you properly so you don't experience any foot pain. If for any reason, and I mean **any** reason, they hurt, return them immediately and try another style.

In addition to comfortable walking shoes, use a pedometer. This little device that you wear on your hip counts how many steps you walk, either during your walk or during the entire day. This is important because regardless of where you walk you can keep track of your time, or how many steps or miles you have taken.

Tracking and monitoring your activity is so important. The goal is 10,000 steps a day. It is also vital to see your progress, to reassure yourself and reinforce that you did it and can continue to do it. Tracking also helps you to be accountable to yourself, to be consistent, and to show how successful you have become. You can keep a log and establish a goal for yourself, see your progress, redefine your goal, and then make this part of your daily routine.*

---

* To order a pedometer or a copy of the activity tracking form, go to www.corporatefitnessworks.com or email Brenda Loube at bloube@corporatefitnessworks.com.

Also, I use a portable radio or Walkman for music – usually oldies but goodies – and I also wear a tune belt, which is like a fanny pack that holds either a Walkman or CD player around my waist. You do not need to hold it in your hand.

The last item I recommend is a water bottle. Remember to drink constantly before, during, and after your walk. You are now ready to move your body and to begin your journey to a healthier you. This is something all of us can aspire to do. The key is to make it a priority and an everyday ritual.

Why do you brush your teeth every day? How did we as children develop this habit? As kids, our parents taught us to brush our teeth both in the morning and at night. Imagine that we were taught to walk a mile before breakfast. Do you think we would still be walking that mile today? There is no question in my mind we would be doing at least two to three times that today as adults.

Get yourself into a routine and stick to it.

Find your passion

To me, physical activity is the foundation for so many things. It helps to build our self-confidence, self-esteem, self-worth, self-respect, and our overall sense of value. It teaches us about loving and caring for ourselves. The challenge is to establish a lifelong ritual that we can incorporate into our lives regardless of the challenges we face. All of us have had life events that have taken us away from doing what is best for us. These challenges happen everyday but do not have to permanently interfere with our daily activity.

As we look at all of our challenges, whether it be projects, business, vacations, family, sickness, or the unexpected surprises, we need not be derailed by them. Instead we need to have a plan to counteract them and prevent these challenges from getting in our way. Just make a conscious decision to get back on track. Give yourself permission for the break and make it OK. Allow the break in your ritual, re-group, remember to get back to your priority and not to punish yourself. It is only a break, not a total interruption in what is important to you.

I realize you must find the passion for yourself. Passion to want the best for yourself, your body, and your health. Passion to reach your potential, so much that you want to do whatever it takes to reach it. I call this Taking Care of Yourself. Our bodies, our internal organs, our systems were designed to be a functional body – one that was made to be active and to move every day. I challenge you to walk daily and make it a commitment for life. I promise your body will look forward to it. I promise you will feel better and be a new person.

So what do you need to motivate yourself to "just move your body" every day for the rest of your life? I have the program. It is called **TME: Thirty Minutes Everyday.** Or how about TME, standing for Time for ME? The challenge is on for you to take these six simple steps to begin your journey of daily physical activity.

Six simple steps to Thirty Minutes Everyday (TME):

1. **Develop a short-term goal:** How much time or how many days per week are you going to commit to being active?

2. **Equipment:** Purchase a comfortable pair of walking shoes, a pedometer to measure your steps and a water bottle and you are ready to go.

3. **Write your daily activity on a calendar:** Write down your goal and check off your daily activity on a calendar or log it in your journal. Put it on your refrigerator or your workstation or bathroom mirror where you can see it every day.

4. **Buddy up:** Find a friend or family member who will join you with your program, someone who will be there for you whether on the walking course or on the phone or both.

5. **Reward yourself:** Think about what you want to give yourself once you reach your first short-term goal. How about a massage? Or a manicure? Even a new pair of walking shoes.

6. **Repeat positive motivational or inspirational sayings:** These affirmations will remind you of your potential. Find or create positive affirmations that work for you. Such as "I can do this and my body loves to move" or "I deserve to feel wonderful."

Now you are ready to play. You have what it takes. You can give yourself permission to make 30 minutes of physical activity a priority, right now, today. It is never too late to begin. Just remember, you can play. Even though I wasn't chosen to play dodge ball with the boys, I didn't let that stand in my way. I eventually proved that I deserved to play. So do you.

Kicked Off the Merry-Go-Round

Jan Richardson, LE (Life Experience)

Jan Richardson traveled the world with her military family during childhood, living in Japan, Taiwan, Idaho, California, Washington, and Oregon, and is now settled in Tigard, Oregon, with her husband, Ron. She has worked as an administrative assistant, legal secretary, office manager, and now owns her own business, providing administrative and marketing support for a variety of entrepreneurs, including Kay Allenbaugh, creator/author of the national best-selling series *Chocolate for a Woman's Soul*; for her husband's business, Ron Can Do It; and for several professional speakers.

Jan is a former professional organizer and was a member of NAPO (National Association of Professional Organizers) and an officer in the Oregon Chapter. She has also been a member of National Speakers Association, Oregon Chapter.

An active volunteer, Jan has been involved with the local Chamber of Commerce as a chairperson and member of numerous committees, founding mother and leader of the Tigard Chamber Women's Business Forum, an officer and board member of her homeowners' association, and a member of the Tigard Mayor's Blue Ribbon Council.

Jan has been redesigning her life since triple bypass surgery in May 2002 and has rediscovered a love for writing, interior decorating, painting, and more. In that pursuit, Jan was recently accepted as a contributing author in a *Chocolate for a Woman's Soul* sequel to be released in 2004 and has been telling her story, "Kicked Off the Merry-Go-Round," to women's groups in her community. She and Ron have three grown daughters, one son, and six grandchildren in their blended family.

Jan Richardson
13367 SW Scotts Bridge Dr.
Tigard, OR 97223
(503) 590-7818
jan@speakersolutions.net

My Story

It sneaked up on me ever so slowly, like a wave, and then, all of a sudden, it landed on me. Oh, I'd noticed that my clothes were fitting a little snugger but, of course, I thought they'd probably shrunk a little during laundering (we fool ourselves in so many ways when we don't want to face the truth). And I realized that I was a little out of breath when I walked up the stairs or went for a walk, but it was only "just a little."

And about that heartburn – last time I had it was when I was pregnant (and I knew I wasn't pregnant!). "Boy, it's hell to get old," I told my peers, as we jokingly compared our latest aches and pains.

I was trying to keep up with the hectic pace of life (yet, I was slowing down), running a business, spending time with family, volunteering, and keeping up with responsibilities at home. So much to do, so little time. I felt like I was on a merry-go-round!

As business partners, my daughter, Tamara, and I were struggling. We'd been working from our separate homes for over a year. In order to be efficient and accessible to our clients, we made the decision to rent office space in July 2000.

We were doing just fine until the economy started hitting the skids. Then our livelihood was further affected by the 9/11 crisis. People quit traveling, conventions were canceled, and the speaking industry took a big hit, drastically affecting our revenue, since our target market was primarily professional speakers/authors. I was under a great deal of stress.

A disagreement with a client about a commission was the incident that took me beyond my ability to cope. Not long after this conflict, I began experiencing neck pain that resembled a "Charlie-horse." Then I began having difficulty breathing and severe pain in my head. I privately denied that these warning signs were anything serious and attributed the discomforts to the stress in my life. I said to myself, "Relax, don't worry, these aches will go away." But they didn't go away. Within the next two weeks, the pains had worsened. I was fearful but didn't want to admit that it might be serious.

During one of the episodes of neck pain and breathing difficulty, my husband took a hard look at my face and took matters into his own hands. "I'm taking you to the ER," he said. I made no protest, secretly relieved that he had made the decision for me.

True to the way things usually work, the pain had subsided by the time we got to the hospital. In spite of that, I submitted to an EKG, blood tests, and long periods of waiting. The doctor finally returned with the results of the tests and said with raised eyebrows, "This is a bit of a surprise." Indeed it was. She admitted me for observation because my heart enzymes were slightly elevated. Elevated heart enzymes? I had heard of this . . . and it scared me to death.

From that point on, everything became a hazy, gray blur. I've tried to remember but I don't recall much of what transpired during the next few days. I was told that the doctors planned to perform an angiogram as well as an angioplasty. But the next morning, 20 minutes into the procedure, the surgeons realized that my condition was worse than they'd expected. A triple bypass was crucial. But it was Memorial Day, and a complete surgical staff was not available, so I was kept sedated until the following morning when the whole operating team would be on deck.

I don't know what transpired during those lost days, but I awoke in the recovery room. And it would be yet another whole week before I could go home to start my healing process. I wasn't complaining. I was grateful. **I got a second chance at life.** I have since learned that most women die in these circumstances. In addition to the heart disease, I was also diagnosed with type II diabetes.

With this second chance to live, I continue to re-evaluate my priorities. I've always coexisted with joy and a positive attitude, but I wasn't taking care of my health. Now, it's imperative that I make sensible life choices because if I don't have my health, I have nothing. Apparently, I needed a "wake-up call." Don't wait until something awful happens. Learn from my experience and take charge of your own life, before it's too late.

The Challenges

When I entered the hospital, life as I knew it, came to a screeching halt.

Suddenly, I was unable to work. I needed help with the simplest tasks, like getting out of bed. I was faced with major lifestyle changes: relearning how to shop for groceries, cook, and eat; making time for regular exercise; resigning from volunteer activities; and closing my business. Tamara tried to keep our business going, but we were already struggling and the task was too difficult. I needed time to recuperate and adjust to the changes.

The Recovery

Without my family and friends, the recovery would have been even more difficult. I spent nine days in the hospital and, thankfully, Tamara stayed with me to make sure I got the care I needed, since Ron was unable to. Being self-employed and now the sole provider, Ron was struggling to keep up with his workload and all the extra responsibilities he had to take on because I was "out of commission."

A blur of people streamed in and out of my room day and night. Someone weighed me every morning, tested my blood every hour, and brought my meds. And I saw a variety of doctors: three different primary care physicians, two cardiologists, my surgeon, a dietician, a wound specialist, my endocrinologist, and a cast of others, not counting a host of nurses who changed every shift.

One of my nurses was memorable. Tyler was the best. He took care of me three days in a row (long shifts), so we had a chance to get acquainted. He made a huge difference in my recovery at "Spa St. Vincent's" (our nickname for the hospital). Tyler was warm, friendly, cute, efficient, and full of fun.

One day, he brought fresh towels and clean "jammies," announcing that it was time to take a shower. I think I was starting to smell a bit. As he helped me to the bathroom, I looked up at him coyly and said, "I used to be pretty hot stuff!" We shared a good laugh, because I certainly didn't look like "hot stuff" at that particular moment with no make-up, my hair flattened to my head, and my tush hanging out. We found something to laugh at each day, and Tyler certainly lifted my spirits. He was one of the many angels in my steady journey toward health.

Once home from the hospital, I had to figure out what I could eat, how food was going to get prepared, who was going to shop for groceries, and how I was going to manage taking nine medications. It was a daunting task. I needed someone to take over the organization and preparation of meals for several weeks – and here I was – a professional organizer in dire need of a plan.

Once again, angels helped me on my way. Friends brought food for us and helped determine what I could eat. I had so many new eating rules that I was afraid to eat anything. We had lots of offers of help, but I still found it difficult to ask.

The first week I was home I felt well, and everybody who came to see me marveled at how good I looked. Tamara was in control of my visitors, and the rule was that they take me on a "stroll" around the cul-de-sac so I could sneak in my exercise. It worked well.

But I felt "crummy" the second week. I had no energy or appetite. I didn't know if this was normal or if something was wrong so I finally called the doctor. He discovered that the cholesterol medications were affecting my liver. Lordy! I had developed drug-induced hepatitis.

I was able to drive by the fifth week. Yea! The doctors had cautioned me that it would take five to six weeks before I would start feeling normal. They were right on target. They also told me that it would take from six months to a year before I was fully recovered from major surgery. On target again! I have learned so much through this journey.

The Aftermath

"Just recovering" from surgery was the easy part. There was so much more to contend with. As a side effect of the anesthetic, I experienced short-term memory loss, an inability to focus my attention, and difficulty in sorting and processing information. Then there was the mountain of paperwork from the insurance company, medical bills, and bills for business expenses, and I had no income to pay them. It was frustrating and discouraging.

Business and personal paperwork began to pile up because I was the one who took care of those things, and I was out of whack. I also received lots of get-well cards, flowers, and gifts, and as much as I loved receiving them, it added to my list of things to do: sending thank you notes to all these wonderful people who cared about me. Keeping track of what I ate and drank, my weight, meds, and my blood glucose level was more than I could handle.

Just as I was starting to regain some energy, and get back into the swing of things, God stopped me from getting on the merry-go-round again. I had an emergency appendectomy on New Year's Eve (I like to liven things up on holidays!). This second surgery took the wind out of my sails and made me realize I had to slow down even more.

Despite the pain and the challenges, through the difficult recovery and adjustment, I still thank God for kicking me off this merry-go-round and for giving me this second chance! Heart surgery has been one of the best things that ever happened to me. I have enjoyed learning about foods that I would never have tried otherwise and I've found that I like them. I have now made exercise a priority and rediscovered a love for writing, cooking, and speaking to women's groups, sharing my story.

I've discovered the importance of "quiet time" – it's when I think and re-energize. I have become closer to my husband and have developed special bonds with new and old friends. I know that my family appreciates me even more. I am grateful for the lessons I have learned through this life-altering experience and would like to share some of those lessons with you.

Kicked Off the Merry-Go-Round

Order out of chaos

Let's hope you don't get kicked off the merry-go-round, as I did. But if life sends you a wake-up call, don't be too hard on yourself and don't expect to "bounce right back." Take care of yourself. I learned how and so can you.

Spend a little time each day or week getting your life in order so that when you encounter a major event in your life (loss of a job, divorce, birth of a child, major illness/accident, or death), you will have some of the basics under control. Good habits and routine help you keep your sanity when life gets crazy. These major events create chaos, and if you feel out of control now, it will add a great deal of stress to your already chaotic life.

Before you have a major life event, put these activities on your to-do list and do them:

- Make sure your Will and Medical Directives are up to date and in order.
- Give a copy to someone you trust, along with names and phone numbers of key people – lawyer, doctors, insurance agents, and other key contacts.
- Your lawyer should have a copy of the Will, the doctors should have copies of your Medical Directives, and your insurance agent should have copies of important insurance papers (health and life).
- Keep copies of important information in a file cabinet in your home, a safety deposit box, and/or in your freezer (for fire safety).
- Build trusting relationships with neighbors and friends (they can be helpful during difficult times). Your family is probably already overwhelmed. Friends and neighbors can help with the following:
    - Picking up your mail/paper if you're out of town
    - Caring for your children, feeding the dog
    - Cooking meals for you and your family

  - Running errands, buying groceries, picking up
    prescriptions

- If your home or office is full of clutter, if you can't find what
  you need in a timely manner, if you don't have room for all
  your "stuff," and if you feel out of control, consider a couple of
  options:
    - Hire a professional organizer, or
    - Ask (bribe) a friend to help you tackle the areas in your
      home that are out of control. Tackle one room at a time
      and one area of the room at a time (you don't have to do
      it all in a day or even a week).
    - Create a plan for getting rid of the stuff you no longer
      want or need.
        - Sort things into paper bags or boxes by category:
          Sell, Donate, Repair, File. Create the categories
          based on your needs.
        - Call charitable organizations (Goodwill, Salvation
          Army, women's shelter) to see if they will pick up
          donated items.

After a major life event, you can gain control of the situation by
doing these activities:

- Create a system of file folders or file box in which to sort your
  medical bills, insurance papers, medical information, and get
  well cards (for sending thank you notes).
- Create a 3-ring binder notebook in which to keep information such as doctors' names and numbers, pharmacy name and
  number, prescription information (name, dose, directions),
  other important phone numbers (friends, neighbors, family,
  employer), information you now need to track (food, weight,
  blood glucose, blood pressure, lab results), and a daily diary of
  how you're feeling.
- Ask for someone's help in determining what your needs will be
  and for approximately how long, such as meal preparation,
  grocery shopping, child care, laundry, and paying bills.

Lessons learned

- If you don't take time to care for yourself, you won't be around to take care of anyone else (because as women, we're always taking care of others).
- Quiet time is very important to re-energize, to solve problems, and be creative.
- Exercise and eating healthy are important – we hear it all the time and keep procrastinating about getting started because we're too busy.
- Take time for what's important and what you really love.
- Life is not a dress rehearsal; we just get one chance so make the most of it.
- Each choice we make has an impact – it could be short term or long term.
- You can't do it all – at the same time!
- Make a concerted effort to get and keep your life in order.
- Get rid of stuff you don't need or want.
- Quit procrastinating and just do it!
- Learn to say NO THANK YOU, I CAN'T DO IT THIS TIME (another opportunity will come along). Remember, if you say no, you are giving someone else a chance.

You Just Need the Right Attitude...
and a Rolex!

Becki Drahota, MBA

Becki Drahota is President and founder of Mills Financial Marketing, a fully integrated resource for banks, credit unions, and companies serving the financial industry. The company was incorporated in 1975 when Becki was 25 years old and currently has net annual billings over $1 million. With clients in a 12-state area, who have assets from $40 million to $1.4 billion, her firm provides market and customer research, strategic planning, creative execution, public relations, and training.

In 1999-2000 she trained over 1,000 Iowa bankers statewide and has been selected by the Iowa Bankers Association to lead a statewide sales training initiative in 2003. She is also a guest lecturer at Buena Vista University and a leadership trainer for the EMBA program at the University of Nebraska-Omaha.

An honors graduate of Drake University and the school's 2001 Distinguished Alumnae recipient, Becki completed her Executive MBA in August 2003 from the University of Nebraska-Omaha with a 4.0 GPA.

Becki was recently appointed as the Honorary Chairman for Iowa for the Republican National Committee's Business Advisory Council. Iowa's Governor appointed her to the Iowa Workforce Council. She was the first woman to be accepted into membership in her Rotary International chapter.

Becki Drahota, MBA
Mills Financial Marketing
612 Seneca St.
Storm Lake, IA 50588
(712) 732-4899
www.millsmarketing.com

My Story

As we lined up for the dinner buffet, one of my classmates turned to me and asked, "Why are you here?" I smiled, and replied honestly. "I'm not sure. I'll let you know when I figure that out."

The same question was posed to me throughout my MBA experience. At 52, most people mistook me for a professor, and no one could figure out why someone who had owned her own business for 27 years would make a substantial investment to sacrifice virtually all non-working hours for two years in the pursuit of finance formulas and term papers boasting footnotes of staggering magnitude.

I was never expected to get an advanced degree. While my brother graduated law school and got a Rolex, I, the journalism major, was supposed to find a job that didn't embarrass my folks. Which I dutifully did, marrying my high school sweetheart and having two daughters along the way.

Early in the marriage I discovered that my husband's "bad boy" behavior while dating had escalated into alcoholism and abuse. As he got fired from job after job, our options narrowed, and he moved us back to our small Midwest town to work for my dad. At the time, I was working for an ad agency and was devastated to leave a job I loved. One of my clients, a large credit union in Denver, suggested I start my own marketing firm. They promised to be my first client. My local bank agreed to be the second. My brother loaned me office space, and on June 1, 1975, at the ripe old age of 25, I incorporated.

Soon after, my husband became virtually unemployable, and I hired him to save face, mostly mine.

Within a few years he abandoned us. My divorce decree stipulated I pay him $3,000 a month for the privilege of keeping my house.

By now I had a payroll to meet, two active daughters to raise, and some serious bills.

My Denver client was key to survival of the company, and it was a good match. They received high-energy creative services and low prices. I learned by doing. Every three weeks for 14 years I would leave home at 4 a.m. – drive to the Sioux City airport and fly to Denver, ready for our marketing meeting at 9, returning on the 6 p.m. flight and arriving home after the 10 p.m. news.

As a mother with a young business and young children, I was chronically short on time and long on fatigue.

In those days, ironing was out of the question. If I stood poised at the dryer, I could snatch my perma-press blouse at the exact post-wrinkle moment, put it on, grab a navy blazer and look passably professional. It was during one of those pre-dawn rituals I forgot to factor static cling and traveled from Iowa to Denver with a pair of nylon underpants adhered to my back.

I have arrived at a meeting to discover I was wearing unmatched shoes. (I bought slippers and feigned foot injury.) I have flown to the wrong Springfield to facilitate a focus group. (Did you know there are 48 Springfields?) I have had to stop at a local hospital to donate breast milk because during a four-hour meeting I was visibly turning into Dolly Parton.

I have also experienced the dark side: A client who insisted on meeting at his hotel "for convenience" and threatening that if I didn't sleep with him, he'd blackball me in the financial community. A now-fired bank president detoured our route to the airport to a motel where he refused to let me out of the car.

And I have been party to the bizarre, particularly cab drivers. Arriving late one Halloween in a new city, I discovered my airport-to-hotel cabbie was a Satan worshipper. It was a pretty big day for him, and he was feeling benevolent, so he gave me a charm that looked like someone's bone, and told me if I threw it away a member of my family would die.

I have lost my luggage and outfitted myself at an all-night Wal-Mart.

I get lost so often I know several of the On-Star reps personally. And I proudly earned the highest GPA in my MBA class while shepherding a small company that bills over $1 million annually and maintains a profit margin of 58 percent.

Pretty heady stuff, at least for a blonde journalism major with no Rolex.

What I want to share is how, as a single mom (now happily married!) my company came to be and how we developed a value proposition that has successfully differentiated our team to the extent that we have no peers. No other company does exactly what we do, and this individuality and focus has allowed us to price relationally. In other words, our output will never be a commodity and because of that there will always be a unique reason for clients to choose us.

We are what we repeatedly do. Excellence then,
is not an act, but a habit.
– Aristotle

You Just Need the Right Attitude . . . and a Rolex!

The green Cadillac

My dad looked a lot like Ichabod Crane. He was tall and lanky, bald, sported a big German nose and was host to a plethora of steel-cased prejudices. One of them was his overall opinion of women, which manifested every time I achieved something worthy enough to tell him. If he approved, his commendation was always accompanied by the status leveler – "for a girl." Which is probably why I became passionately competitive to achieve what I felt was his level of success.

Dad always drove a Cadillac, the bigger the better. Foreign cars were Communist, and smaller cars lacked the panache of a living room on wheels.

So when my company began to experience modest success, the first thing I did was purchase an emerald-green Fleetwood, super-sized.

On my maiden voyage to Des Moines, a three-hour trip, the weather was lousy. Although there was blowing snow, ice, and frightening wind chills, I was smug in my wire-rimmed "successory." Until the computerized "brain" malfunctioned. The temperature inside the car soared to 102 degrees, regardless of what button I pushed. I was forced to roll down the windows and drive with snow melting my heavily sprayed "do" and washing mascara down my cheeks.

I got in the car looking like a junior executive. I got out of the car looking like Alice Cooper.

Life's lesson: My dad's manifestations of success didn't have to be mine. No one except **you** should define yourself.

The bridge too strong to burn

For years our company has had the good fortune to work for a large – and growing – financial institution in Colorado. Their billings were pretty close to critical mass for me and my team.

As my client reached the billion-dollar milestone in assets, they began to upgrade their management and re-evaluate old partnerships. Since we qualified as an old partner, they graciously offered us the opportunity to keep their business. We presented with fervor (and a little panic). While other agencies wined and dined them, we had to drive them from the Sioux City airport two hours to our small Iowa town, with nothing more enchanting than soybean fields and the unmistakable "smell of money" (that's manure to you city folk) to amuse them.

They were gracious. They were kind. They fired us. They felt although we had great skills, they needed a new level of expertise to take them into the future. I was deeply saddened to lose the relationship, but I understood. Had I been in their shoes, I might have done the same thing.

So I told them the truth: Their friendship was just as important as their business. We helped their new agency get acclimated and offered our help if they got in a crunch.

One evening two months later, at home with a modestly priced merlot in hand, I answered the phone. It was 6:30 p.m., and we were just sitting down for dinner. On the line was our former client, who after apologizing for calling me at home said, "We made a mistake. Can you start working for us tomorrow?"

It was the best glass of merlot I've ever tasted.

Life's lesson: Respect is at the core of every long-term success. Don't burn a bridge that could lead someone back to you.

Take that, Dr. Laura!

I'm a working mom. I have always **had** to be and **wanted** to be. When my daughters were small, we had a ritual every morning: I would stand at the door and they would cling to my legs and ask me not to go. I would hug them, kiss them and lament, "Mommy has to go to work. I'm so sorry."

All of us started the day with sadness, and I added a huge scoop of guilt. The guilt was a result of my childhood experiences. My mother was 40 when I was born, so I was shamelessly doted upon. For example, while my second-grade classmates unwrapped blue Kleenexes with crumbled Oreos at milk time, I would come in from recess to a warm, homemade cinnamon roll on my desk. It's amazing I didn't get beaten up. My value system was this: "Good" moms stayed home with their kids.

So I'd go to the office each morning and lament that I wasn't at home. If I'd go home early, I'd fret about all the work that wasn't getting done at the office. I managed to make **all** of us miserable for part of the day and myself miserable for most of it.

One morning, as I wiped Abby's tears, I realized I was lying to my girls. Although I'd miss them terribly, I was looking forward to the events of that day, not dreading them. So I fessed up.

"Honey," I explained, "I love you more than anything in the world. And I will miss you. But I'm not sad to go to work. I'm proud of what I do, and I enjoy doing it."

Abby's tears stopped. She stepped back from my leg and said, "I thought you'd feel badly if I didn't cry. Now I don't have to. Bye, mom!" And with that she turned back to her Barbies.

I know that I'm not a perfect parent. Far from it. But I also know I'm a good mom. For the small price of a little less sleep each night, I have had a successful career and a richly rewarding family life.

My job teaches me how and allows me to support my daughters' aspirations and open doors for them through travel and unique experiences. My children teach me balance (problems at work are important, but not critical) and how to manage my time.

It is a symbiotic relationship.

Life's lesson: You can't have it all, but most of life's choices aren't 100 percent mutually exclusive either. Diversify your life for the same reason you diversify your investment portfolio – to keep yourself balanced.

Quickies

- Long before Jim Collins published the book *Good to Great* with his hedgehog management theory, we had our 10 Expectations of Professionalism. Number 4 is "Do most what you do best." Every time we've wandered afield of this maxim, we've lost money. **Every** time.
- Another expectation is "Use your own best judgment at all times." If you have a good team, that's all the management criteria you need. The rest is coaching.

Life's lesson: Be opinionated. Be passionate. And be a grown-up. Accept each assignment as though your job depended on it, and put a piece of yourself into everything you do. That way you'll never produce junk.

More quickies

- Recently a client asked my art director why she had stayed with me 20 years. "I may have worked for the same company," she replied. "But I've had four different careers here."
- Introducing me at a luncheon, one of my account execs once said, "Working for Becki is like jumping out of a plane every morning. You've packed your parachute, but you always wonder if it will open."

Life's lesson: It's OK to be afraid. But it's not OK to let fear stop you.

The Plumeria syndrome

Did I mention that until early 2003, my company was composed of all women? While certainly not a strategy in my business plan, the team, for most of its 27-year history, has been female.

During my first decade as CEO, dishwasher, and garbage-hauler, most of my client contact was with bank or credit union presidents. Marketing, my area of expertise, was still considered an expense as opposed to an investment, and I had to fight hard to achieve credibility. So I became "The Agenda Nazi." Barely allowing myself time to exchange greetings, I conducted our regular conferences by ruthlessly pursuing the tasks at hand, always suggesting we forgo lunch to work "efficiently."

Looking back, I tried to achieve parity by performance and affectations. They smoked. I smoked. Sort of. I'd light a Silva Thin and gesture grandly with one poised between my manicured nails until the burning tip fell off, usually on the table. I drank gallons of mud-thick caffeinated coffee, black, until once again I started becoming Dolly Parton, this time as an allergic reaction to caffeine. (Note to small-busted women: Do not try this as a cheap breast enhancement. It hurts *unbelievably.*)

I drank Bloody Marys at lunch. Once. Let your imagination finish this one.

My comeuppance came when it was time to renew a contract with one of my South Dakota banks. The president said he'd continue our relationship only on the condition that I took one hour for lunch per meeting, at a restaurant, and talked during that time like a human being, not a robot. So I responded by going overboard – in the opposite direction.

My second decade was punctuated by big blonde hair, pink ultrasuede suits, and briefcases that cost more than the rent on my first apartment. I also, because of working really long days, layered my scent. I used Bath & Body Works Plumeria shower gel, followed by body lotion, layered with body splash and topped off with scented lip gloss.

I was a bordello with a briefcase. Again, it was a client, this time in Missouri, who initiated the reality check. When he popped his head in the conference room at one meeting I asked, "How did you know I was here today?" "I smelled you," he said. "The whole floor smelled you."

Middle age and moderate success have allowed me to enter my third decade with more balance. But I *do* have a really great pair of Burberry plaid pumps!

Life's lesson: You are a businesswoman. Be both. Be real.

——— ◆ ———

"So why **are** you here?" asked another MBA student. You don't **need** this degree to keep your job. Why not save the money? Why not travel? Relax? Retire?

The answer is that I had gotten as smart as I was going to get. I couldn't run my company better or continue to role model for my kids until I knew more. And if I knew more, I could do more.

It took 30 years to get my graduate degree. Along the way I have been lucky enough to help raise two extraordinary daughters and be a part of an extraordinarily professional team.

I got my MBA. And a Rolex. To remind me the timing of my life's events may not be perfect, but every moment is a treasure. And to annoy my brother the lawyer.

My bottom line: These are the maxims that govern our team and our company. Help yourself.

10 Expectations of Professionalism

1. Stop worrying about what everyone else is doing.
2. Use your own best judgment at all times.
3. Help each other.
4. Do most what you do best
5. Remember, the customer is the boss.
6. Don't ask for help until you've tried it yourself.
7. If you backbite, expect to get bit back.
8. Respect each other.
9. Care about what you do.
10. Believe in what we are doing.

Be An Attitude Leader

Nora Butcher, MSW

A leader in the human development area, Nora Butcher has mastered a variety of challenges through professional speaking, teaching, coaching, and psychotherapy. With her warmth, intelligence, humor, and caring, she easily builds rapport with different ages and groups from teens at Amistad Academy to CEOs.

Nora is a motivational speaker and leads self-discovery seminars. She is a member of the National Speakers Association, National Association of Social Workers, Toastmasters International, and ASTD. She holds a master's degree cum laude from Michigan State University and bachelor's degree from Aquinas College. She resides in Michigan with her family and grandchildren. She lives with passion while coaching and coaxing you to let your creative spirit shine.

Nora Butcher, MSW
Corporate Coaching Associates
www.norabutcher.com
www.attitude-leaders.com

Nora Butcher

Attitude leaders have passion and purpose.
Attitude leaders are inner directed.
Attitude leaders make a place for power.

My Story

My father never lost his dream despite the dangers of war. The same morning I was born, he shipped out from New York destined for the battlefields of World War II. Surrounded by fear, destruction, and death, he carried a picture of his family. He returned a year and a half later carrying ghosts from the war yet with his dreams and optimistic spirit intact.

Both he and my mother were hard-working people. My mother's motto was "God helps them who help themselves." So we all worked. Hoed gardens, fed chickens, picked strawberries, raspberries, corn, and beans and canned vegetables. I had a "pickle patch." All summer on my hands and knees, I picked pickles to get money for the family and for "travlin' shoes." ("All God's children need travlin' shoes" – Maya Angelou)

Coming up from that pickle patch, I learned planning, persistence, perseverance, a positive attitude, and work. After graduating salutatorian from high school, I went on to college. My academic advisor ignored all the prerequisites and put me in History of Modern Philosophy because she thought it would complement the Modern Novel class she'd picked for me.

Fr. Ricardo, the philosophy professor, was gruff and spoke with a heavy Cuban accent. Imagine a stauncher and stricter Rickie Ricardo teaching Machiavelli and Sartre. I studied all night for the midterm, which was the first test. The morning of the exam Fr. Ricardo wrote three questions on the board and said, "Answer one of these in detail." Anyway, that's what I thought he said.

I wrote furiously for an hour and a half until he collected the papers. Walking down the hall, I asked my friend Carole, "Which one did you answer?" She said, "What do you mean 'which one'? I answered all of them." Now in panic, I whirled around and searched for Fr. Ricardo. Panting I explained what had happened. He bellowed, "You flunk!" and turned and strode away.

Silently I cried during my next class. Then I said firmly, "You can't flunk! Go and talk to him." Fearfully I dragged myself to his office, explained what had happened and asked to discuss the possibilities. When he discovered this was my first philosophy class, his arms flailed, anger exploded from his ears and nostrils as well as his mouth. After he settled down and noticed that I was still there, he gave me a pile of books to read and told me to report on them. Every two weeks he received a report on one of the books.

This pattern of "bouncing back" with an optimistic spirit recurs throughout my life regardless of circumstances. I have a passion for seeing the possibilities. I prefer it to picking pickles in the 92-degree heat. My optimism helps people uncover their inner, hidden strengths. I want to help you uncover your passion and possibilities. Let me share what I have learned that will point a way for you to follow your path.

Are you an attitude leader? You need passion and purpose to be an attitude leader. What ignites your passion? Your heart's desire? This is your entelechy [your reason for being] . . . your uniqueness. It burns within and yearns to be realized. The world needs your passion as much as you need to live it.

When your path follows your passion, you know where you are going. When you haven't found your path, you put obstacles in your way. For example, if you are in a job that you don't want, you may go to work with a disgruntled attitude and spread negativity. You sabotage yourself and your work.

Plan your true path. Uncover the patterns in your life. What did you enjoy as a child? What have you always wished to do but couldn't because of responsibilities? What do you daydream? What are your lost dreams?

If you can identify with this, I would like to help you. Let me share what I have learned on this path.

Be An Attitude Leader

Attitude leaders are inner directed

It's about psychology. You don't fail because you can't accomplish or aren't smart enough. You fail because you don't understand this process and get off track or discouraged.

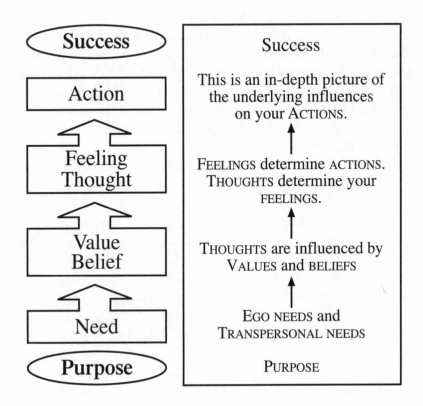

Power of purpose

We all want meaning and purpose in our lives and in our work. Are you living from your unique purpose? We've already discussed the importance of your purpose. Now it's time to identify your purpose. Write it here: _____

_____

_____

_____

This becomes the foundation of your contract with yourself.

Power of needs

Whenever you experience strong feelings, they indicate your unmet underlying needs. Divide this circle into five parts to represent your mental, physical, social, emotional, and spiritual needs. The size of the slice indicates the importance you give it. Label and color each slice.

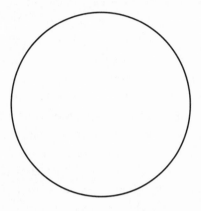

Reflect on the balance or lack of balance you observe. Which needs are not met? Write what you will do here: _____

_____

_____

_____

_____

_____

Power of values and beliefs

Identify your personal beliefs. What do you value: truth, honesty, trustworthiness, caring, flexibility, creativity, gratitude. Add any others here: _____
Your values and beliefs fuel your thoughts.

Power of thoughts

It's not events but the thoughts you have about them that determine whether they have a positive or negative effect on your life. You try to consciously think positive thoughts about achieving your goals. But negative thoughts slightly below the surface challenge and defeat you.

Be aware! Recently Maria saw her book on the bestseller list in the newspaper. Her first words were, "I can't believe it." Her words reveal her unconscious thoughts. Be aware of your thoughts.

Try this. The next time you receive an unexpected acclamation or award, notice your thoughts. Are they positive? Or like Maria do you say, "Oh, I can't believe it!" Don't let them defeat you. Replace your negative thoughts with thoughts that are more realistic.

By the time you were three years old, you had introjected what adults told you. If they said, "Good for you," or "That's okay, you'll do better next time," that's what you're telling yourself today. Too often their comments were critical even though their intention was to help you. If they were critical, you are critical of yourself.

As adults, we must now be aware of our negative thoughts and change them to words that make us strong. Those negative thoughts are based on the judgment of a three-year-old. They were erroneous at the time and still are today. It's time to rid your mind of the negative chatter and make room for thoughts of success: faith, hope, and love.

Eliminate excuses: "If only . . ." They keep you in the past and cause failure. Banish blame: "I could have . . . I should have . . . would have . . . " This causes failure. Until you change your negative self-talk, you look outside yourself for approval: "Am I good enough?" "Do you approve?" Negative thoughts are habits you can change in the present.

When I first started professional speaking, if I made a mistake, I calmed myself by saying, "It's okay. It's only one small part. Look at the big picture. Good for you . . . you faced your fears. You'll do better next time." I move my ego to the side, passionately present the best I can, and keep learning from mistakes.

Power of feelings

"It's not that I don't want to feel. It's just that I don't want to be there when it happens," may reflect how you feel about strong emotions. You may fear you'll be overwhelmed, go out of control or do something illogical. You may feel you are just surviving day to day and decide it's best to ignore feelings. Maybe they'll go away.

Guess what? Feelings can't be ignored. Just as a crying baby gets louder and louder when ignored, your feelings get louder. They turn up as nightmares, as mental or physical illness. But if you console the crying baby and say, "There, there, it's okay," the baby stops crying. Care for your feelings, accept and express them appropriately.

Warnings:

- Don't try to eliminate a feeling intellectually by thinking about "why" you have it. Such thinking only derails you.
- Don't repress feelings. Such practice is psychologically and medically unwise.
- Rampant emotional expression is not acceptable.

Feelings are part of what makes us human. The path to inner peace and harmony is through feelings. This is the key. It opens the doors to creativity, spontaneity, joy, playfulness, and inner wisdom. Identify your feelings. Check with yourself several times a day. Ask yourself,

- "It is 10 a.m., what am I feeling?"
- "It is 3:30 p.m., what am I feeling?"
- "It is 9:30 p.m., what am I feeling?"

Draw a symbol to represent your feelings. Use colors and forms. Feelings are not thoughts. If you can replace "I feel ____" with "I think _____" then it's not a feeling, it is a thought.

Sometimes you don't know what you are feeling. Express it anyway. You can express your feelings physically, verbally, in writing, drawing, or moving to music. In hindsight, after you have lived through the experience, you will be able to identify the feeling.

Feelings reside in your body. If you can't find a name for your feeling, ask yourself, "Where do I feel tension in my body?" Describe that area. What shape does it have? How large is it? What color is it? Draw it. Sculpt it in the air in front of you. Write about it. Talk with a trusted friend.

All feelings are part of being human. Any feeling that you can imagine, you experience because you are human. Sometimes people "pick and choose" the feelings they think are acceptable. They push the others to the side. They say, "Rage? No, that's not me, I'm a nice person." Or "Wimpy? Not me, I'm a strong person." "Sad? Not me, I'm a happy person."

What happens to those feelings that get pushed to the side?

- When you deny your feelings, you push them down, repress them and get farther and farther away from knowing yourself and your underlying needs, from knowing "who you are."

- But strong feelings don't stay repressed for long. They push out. At an unexpected point, you "act out" of that repressed feeling, inappropriately, and can't understand why you did that.
- Unexpressed feelings can trigger other feelings. Intense stress for a long period of time can become depression. Unexpressed anger can turn into anger toward yourself and become depression.

Don't let emotions block you! Anger. Revenge. Bitterness. Helplessness. Lethargy. Rage. Unforgiveness. These emotions can consume your energy and block your success. Use the following exercise for any strong feelings that are blocking you. Here's an example using anger.

List beliefs that fuel feeling:	Where did this belief come from?	How can I change it?	What will I do to change it?	When will I change it?
People are out to get me.				
It's their fault.				
I can't do anything about my anger.				
I am just an angry person.				
He makes me angry.				

Beliefs that deny feeling.	Where did this belief come from?	How can I change it?	What will I do to change it?	When will I change it?
I shouldn't be angry.				
I'll lose control.				
Nice people don't get angry.				
Bad things happen when people get angry.				
If I'm angry, it'll be worse.				

Lifeguard view

When you experience feelings, imagine you are a strong lifeguard seated high above, observing your pool of feelings. You can view your feelings from here and know that you are more than your feelings. Give yourself permission to express your feelings honestly.

Build your emotional strength by practicing this strategy daily:

1. What am I feeling?
2. Where do I feel tension in my body?
3. How can I express this feeling appropriately? In writing, movement, drawing, talking? (Caution: Don't just think about feelings! Do not ask "**Why** do I feel this way?" The "why" question takes you to your thinking and away from your feelings. Feelings aren't logical. They don't make any sense.) Just express them appropriately. Then they aren't inside of you, they are out here where you can view them more objectively. If you keep them inside and think about them, you go round and round in circles.
4. What do I need? Underlying any strong feelings are unmet needs. Use logical thinking to problem-solve ways to meet your needs.
5. What thoughts do I choose?

Inner-directed people see the immense beauty and potential within the Self. Your self-esteem and confidence are high because you look to yourself for approval. You lavish support and encouragement on yourself. You have the courage to make decisions.

In *Power Vs Force* David Hawkins, MD, reveals in a map of consciousness the effects of our thoughts and emotions on personal power. The critical level for personal power is courage. The emotion at this level is affirmation through empowerment. All of the egocentric states below courage (pride, anger, desire, fear, grief, apathy, guilt, and shame) make you weak. Tame your ego! It is critical if you want personal power.

Through research Hawkins measured states of consciousness. His studies indicate that positive thoughts make you strong. Courage makes you strong. Fear makes you weak. Monitor and change your thoughts to positive thoughts. This is crucial for success.

Love, compassion, and forgiveness are empowering. Consciously choose a kind approach to life. Be positive about yourself and your life. It will give you more energy, strength, and better health.

Power of action

Attitude leaders are everywhere. I can tell you story after story of attitude leaders who have followed their unique pathway. But I want to help you follow your path. Maybe you know your path but are afraid to follow it. What scares you about achieving it? Are you concerned about what other people think? Are people discouraging you? Are you discouraging yourself?

What gives you passion and power? What is your purpose? Follow your unique pathway.

- Identify inner thoughts and feelings to develop ego strengths.
- Do not compare yourself with others.
- Release negative thoughts of self-invalidation and criticism.
- Embrace your entelechy (your uniqueness).

Attitude leaders make a place for power

If you want power in your life, you have to make a place for power. Your journal maps your journey and keeps you on your path. What do you want to celebrate one year from today? What steps do you need to begin today?

1. Contract with your inner Self. Write your contract on the first page of your journal. Write your purpose.
2. Draw a picture of the person you will be one year from today. Each morning look at this picture.
3. Dream in detail what you want.
4. Choose one small thing that you can do daily. Record it in your journal. Do this every day for 21 days. When it becomes a habit, choose another action.
5. Write a word to guide you today. Each evening recap the day and write your insights.
6. Connect with people. List people who give you positive support. Choose nurturing people.
7. Celebrate the little steps.

When your picture gets torn and frayed, and when you're stumbling and discouraged, remember your purpose and tap into your deep feelings for what this picture means to you personally.

The greatest discovery of our generation
is that human beings
by changing the inner attitudes of their minds,
can change the outer aspects of their lives!

– William James, American psychologist

Be an Attitude Leader. Be Aware in the World.

The Spirit Survives —
Dazed and Unleashed

Deborah Ellenberg, MS

Deborah Ellenberg is a health promotion consultant and physical activity advocate. Her proactive nature and high energy are reinforced by her personal conviction to pursue a vision of excellence in the art of living while helping others do the same. Debbie holds an MS degree from the University of Delaware in health promotion with a concentration in business.

Debbie consults with organizations to enhance health and productivity. Her work involves assessing workplace policy and environmental determinants of health, along with proposal writing, public relations, public speaking, and development, implementation, and evaluation of health promotion programs. She is an adjunct faculty member at Wilmington College (Wilmington, Delaware) and a certified group exercise instructor. Debbie balances her work life with community service involvement, an appreciation of the arts, and participation in daily physical activity. She is an active member of the West Chester Rotary Club, is currently enrolled in an acting class, and enjoys long walks with her dog, Tonic.

Deborah Ellenberg

Deborah Ellenberg, MS
45 May Apple Drive
Downingtown, PA 19335
d_ellenberg@hotmail.com
(610) 269-3946

My Story

My parents have always referred to me as their "free spirit." I was given this title based on a seemingly over-abundance of creative energy coupled with an independent and sometimes stubborn-minded freedom of thought. As a free-spirited adult, I have learned that my frequent nature to challenge assumptions, create alternatives, and follow through on new actions has enabled me to live life to the fullest. Hence, entrepreneurial endeavors and opportunities for the spotlight have always grabbed my attention. Personally and professionally speaking, I believe that life is full of obstacles, challenges, opportunities, and rewards – and it's what we make of it. I have learned that stressful times may daze the spirit but not destroy it. A free spirit means that it is unleashed; therefore it is dynamic, constantly evolving, and builds in strength during times of upheaval.

I'll never forget the day my life seemed to take a detour. It was Dec. 14, 2001. My husband of three years and significant other of additional seven announced, "My feelings for you are dead." Deflecting the harshness of the meaning of words with humor, I replied, "So . . . I should give you mouth-to-mouth, right?" His eyes looked away and with little emotion, I heard the word "no." Six days later, my two-year study working with the American Cancer Society ended. I was prepared for the end of the study but not the marriage. My plans for the Christmas holiday were changed abruptly as feelings of bewilderment, betrayal, and despair tainted the festivities. On December 27, my birthday, my father informed me that my grandfather was admitted into an intensive care unit and "things didn't look good." He passed away shortly thereafter. My New Year's resolutions were replaced with a survival "to do" list: Find full-time employment with benefits, file divorce papers, pack and relocate, and buy a new house.

I was a woman on a mission to regain a sense of control and

happiness. I threw myself into the employment search as if "prospective job hunter" was an official job title accompanied by a 50-hour work week. With the assistance of the University of Delaware's employment counseling and career placement services, I learned effective strategies for job searching and interviewing. During the job search, I was scheduled to teach a course entitled Wellness in the Workplace at Wilmington College. It seemed ironic at the time. Who was I to teach a wellness course when my life was falling apart? I decided to view the opportunity to educate and inspire a class on wellness concepts and the benefits of worksite health promotion programs as an outlet to rekindle my passion. Within three months, I was entertaining two job offers.

I accepted a position with a company located in West Chester, Pennsylvania, and commuted an hour to work for the first four months. The days were long and stressful. I was functioning in survival-mode, averaging 15-hour days between commuting, working, house hunting, and walking my dog. During the week of July 12, I found a townhome and placed a bid, my application for a mortgage was approved, I located a temporary dwelling that allowed big dogs, and my divorce was finalized. While I was making headway on my "to do" list, the chronic stress was starting to take its toll. A past foot injury had flared, which resulted in two stress fractures. I relocated into the temporary one-bedroom efficiency 10 days later, foot in cast.

Although blurred, I was starting to visualize the possibilities and opportunities of change. On Friday, Aug. 23, 2002, I signed the settlement papers on my new house and then drove to my hometown to join in the celebration of my sister's wedding rehearsal dinner. The wedding was Saturday. The next morning I drove back to Downingtown and moved into my new home with the help of a few friends. It was a perfect weekend filled with family, best friends, new beginnings, and an unleashed spirit. I started over.

The Spirit Survives—Dazed and Unleashed

From Survival to Revival:
Steps to Reframe, Research, and Write

Moving from survival mode to revival mode, which I describe as, "alive, revived, and well," requires action steps. Intellectualizing this matter, stress is defined as the subjective experience to events, people, places, situations, or demands – otherwise known as the stressors. The overload of stress is based on your own perspective, the number of stressors, and the level of control you think you have. Research indicates that chronic stress overload and strain results in long-term negative health effects. Logically, if you take action to manage the stress, you can change the outcome.

My advice to anyone who has felt before or will ever feel again the challenges of starting over, as I did, can be boiled down into three significant life-changing steps: reframing, researching, and writing. These three action steps have been invaluable for my personal transformation from survival to revival and, as I have found, are applicable from a personal as well as professional standpoint.

Reframing

Reframing how a situation is viewed in order to manage the stress level is a useful coping mechanism and a wellness concept. Studies show that psychological factors, such as reframing, play a role in enhancing our immune system. Humor and creativity enable us to cope by focusing on the good, the humorous, and allow us to look for the possible benefits, as opposed to concentrating on what causes us emotional distress. Bottom line: Our physiology is affected by the way we react to the situations we perceive as stressful.

By making lemonade out of lemons, we rekindle the energy to maintain and sustain. Let me clarify this statement by sharing an example from my story regarding the temporary dwelling. Since my bid was accepted on the townhome and the efficiency unit was extremely small, the majority of my possessions were placed into storage until I could move from one to the other. This one-room, unfurnished efficiency unit had no air-conditioning and slanted floors. I took clothes for three weeks, a set of bathroom towels, a coffee pot and toaster, one pot for cooking, one place setting including a glass and mug, an air mattress, an ironing board and iron, one dining room chair, a portable radio with CD player, a handful of CDs and magazines, my plants, my dog and cat, and three fans, which ran 24/7 because the heat and humidity were at times unbearable. The ironing board served the dual role as kitchen table/ workstation.

Much to coworkers' dismay, the experience was fondly referred to and remembered as "Camp Minor," thanks to my sister. She helped me reframe the situation by viewing the temporary stay like a camping retreat. Ironically, the efficiency unit was located on Miner Street – so, like the street name, this temporary stay was no big deal.

Reframing the situation creates a buffer effect to stress. For instance, individuals who work in positions where they deal with life and death on a regular basis, such as a police or emergency room staff, are often masters of reframing. This survival mechanism enables them to perform their tasks at hand and not succumb to feelings of insanity or anguish. The beauty of reframing is that it is a skill that requires a mental shift and may be developed, learned, and practiced at any age. You can develop your reframing skills in many ways. Consider the following:

1. **Tap into support networks such as friends and family members to help provide insight during difficult times.** Consider those individuals whom you confide in and evaluate if they have your best interest at heart. If cynicism and negativism seem to be the overriding theme of the advice given, seek out support from personal coaches, therapists, inspirational leaders, and role models. Personal coaches, counselors, and therapists are professionally trained in asking effective questions in order to resolve problems and to help you reflect on the situation. Inspirational leaders and role models include those in the clergy, teachers, and professors and colleagues whom you admire. Expressing the emotion and frustration and disclosing information to supportive others helps to nullify the bottling and internalizing of stress.

2. **Broaden your perspective with the help of books and audiotapes.** There are no fees attached to stopping by the public library, investigating the selections available, and reserving a book or audio series on tape or CD. The authors provide facts and share suggestions on views, which you may have never considered before. If lack of time for reading a book is an obstacle, then try an audio series and listen while performing other activities such as driving, cleaning, or taking

a walk. For example, the Nightingale-Conant Corporation is a credible source of various self-help tapes.

3. **Positively change your physiology by engaging in regular physical activity.** Evaluate your health behavior practices under high levels of stress and assess the impact on your reframing abilities. Inactivity, poor eating habits, sleep deprivation, and substance abuse negatively affect your physical and emotional states, as well as impact your ability to perform and think at optimal levels. Are you incorporating 30 to 60 minutes of physical activity throughout your day? Do you gravitate toward comfort foods that are calorie-dense and high in fat and sugar when stressed? Is your bedroom conducive for restful sleeping? Have you noticed an increase in alcohol consumption or cigarette smoking? Recognize that we can "alter our states" with positive changes in any of these health habits.

Focusing exclusively on the relationship between physical activity and stress, studies show us that individuals who are physically active on a regular basis manage stress levels better than those who are inactive. The reason is that participating in physical activities actually stresses the body. This activity conditions the body to respond to the added energy demands with the release of endorphins. Endorphins are hormones that, when released, positively affect our moods and relax the body. The body doesn't recognize or distinguish "what" the demand or stress is, it is just conditioned to respond with the release of mood-altering hormones.

The American Heart Association recommends 30 to 60 minutes of daily physical activity, which can be accomplished through 10-minute bouts of accumulated activity. Unfortunately, according to the National Center for Chronic Disease Prevention and Health Promotion, 74 percent of American adults are not regularly physically active. Defining physical activity into three categories – formal, fun and functional – may be one strategy for sneaking and scheduling activity into your day.

- Formal activities are the traditional, structured exercise routines, such as weight training or running, that most people typically consider when physical activity is suggested.
- Fun activities are identified as recreational sports we engage in such as rollerblading, hiking, and childhood games and play.
- Functional activities are defined as those ordinary activities such as loading, lifting, shoveling, walking versus driving, taking the steps versus the elevator, and so on.

Think outside the "formal activity box" and use fun and functional strategies to improve your mood and enhance your health.

Researching

Learning how to reframe a stressful situation opens the door for seeing the opportunities that lie within or beyond. Use your energies to investigate and research the potential opportunities. You'll find meaningfulness and purposefulness in that task. I have found that researching the options and opportunities that exist is similar to that of conducting a needs assessment. Understanding the needs, problems, and challenges of the potential opportunities enables you to create and implement solution strategies for quality-of-life issues. Whether the needs assessment is conducted for personal or professional reasons, the first three steps of a needs assessment are applicable for both.

1. **Assess the situation and identify the information, which is needed for "the investigation."** What major concerns do you have that impact your personal well-being? In other words, put on the "Columbo" cap and ask yourself, "How can I get through this situation without losing my sanity?" The answer provides the framework to steps, which are measurable and doable. For example, changing status from married to single, job-hunting, relocating and house hunting were new experiences for me. In an effort not to become overwhelmed, the information that was needed for each task was outlined into small, doable, and effective action steps.

2. **Identify the facts that support the issue, challenge, or problem.** What is the purpose for the needs assessment and how might this purpose benefit others? This homework phase of the needs assessment includes gathering statistics, related-trend highlights, and factors resulting from the issue, challenge, or problem. It provides the "meat on the bones" for generating solution strategies to move forward and create positive changes in your life and the lives of others. This research step also arms you with the ammunition to effectively negotiate, propose, request, and recommend. In my particular situation, I possessed specialized skills, a master's degree in health promotion and flexibility to move and work anywhere. I felt I would be valuable in many work settings simply because obesity is a national epidemic, and sedentary lifestyles are prevalent.

3. **Create a list of the "key informants" and conduct an information interview.** Key informants are the individuals, organizations, and associations you should contact for gathering additional information for your investigation. While it's not necessary and often unlikely that you know the key informant prior to interviewing, you do need to be prepared when querying. When developing questions, remember the objective, because the information you gather is only as good as the quality of the questions you ask. Anticipate possible responses and consider how you might follow up. As a general rule of thumb, an effective line of questioning includes questions that are general to specific, open-ended, probing, and respectful. Your role as interviewer is to actively listen to learn and gather as much information relevant to the reason for the questions.

For example, the study with American Cancer Society resulted out of my need for graduate school funding and the desire to infuse an ACS youth program into the curriculum within schools in Delaware. In the spring of 1999, I was working with ACS to promote one of their youth health promotion programs. During that time, I learned that plans were being made to launch another youth program, which encouraged physical activity and healthy eating. I was intrigued by the program and believed a connection existed to link both programs together and market more effectively. However, I needed more information about the particulars of this new program. I tracked down the program creators and then contacted them. I inquired about the program development, implementation, and evaluation processes. I asked questions such as, "Can you tell me why the program was created?" "How was the program marketed?" and "How were instructors recruited?" Gathering that initial information led to further investigations with other "key informants" and eventually gave me an idea for a marketing plan for program infusion and graduate school funding.

Writing

If you believe that inspiration develops out of desperation, then the final step from survival to revival is the act of writing. It will require you to take action as opposed to taking no action and wallowing in sadness. Use the information you have gathered to write a proposal, submit a request, complete an employment application, or compose a story. These steps are logical, action-oriented, positive, and empowering. For some, this step may be the hardest because this is the point where we are most vulnerable to criticism, rejection, or refusal. On the flip side, this is the stage where we regain a sense of purpose and pride, and we can experience the feeling of accomplishment.

If the possibility of a negative response is holding you back from engaging in this behavior, start by creating your list of perceived benefits. Second, identify the list of perceived barriers and then practice reframing. For instance, consider the following objections:

1. **I don't know what to write about.** Review the information you have gathered during the needs assessment phase. Revisit the purpose and clarify the benefits to others.

2. **I don't have anything worthwhile to write.** The word write refers to many types of writing projects. This includes, but is not limited to, completing an application for a job or mortgage; writing a proposal for grant funding; pitching an idea such as a column for a local paper; composing a story for a chapter in a

book or writing an entire book; or simply scripting your thoughts in a private journal for your own personal reflection.

3. **It might be rejected.** You have nothing to lose and everything to gain. The worst-case scenerio is that your submission will be declined. A rejection letter is an opportunity to edit and revise.

4. **I'm not a skillful writer.** Writing is a skill that is developed and refined through practice. There are many ways to hone your writing skills, which are inexpensive and non-threatening. Consider taking a creative writing class offered by lifelong learning programs. Or consult colleagues, former teachers, and friends for editing advice and feedback.

5. **I don't have time or the energy.** Is this a legitimate excuse or a form of procrastination? Unless a deadline is announced, your time frame is only self-imposed.

6. **My ideas are ridiculous.** The ideas may seem ridiculous or innovative, unique and meaningful to others. Constructive feedback will present opportunities to revise, restructure, and reprint.

7. **I don't know how a proposal is formatted.** Depending on what is being written, format recommendations may be provided by the intended reader with a simple request. For example, grants usually follow a template that includes an executive summary; the statement of need; a description of the project goals, objectives and activities; a projected budget; information about your organization; and a conclusion.

Reframing, researching, and writing are action steps that will require you to change your current behavior. Although these are not health behavior changes, the action step tools may positively impact your overall well being. For more information on adopting a new habit, I highly recommend the book or audio series entitled, *Changing for Good* by James Prochaska, Carlo DiClemente, and John Norcross.

Tim Robbins' character in the movie *Shawshank Redemption* says, "Get busy living or get busy dying." I believe these words provide inspiration and help clarify our basic quality-of-life options. In the face of forced change in our lives, we can choose to physically, mentally, and emotionally shut down, thereby allowing the pain and hurt to completely immobilize us; or we can take a deep breath, feel the emotion, and take action. Revive your spirit by learning to reframe, use your investigative skills to research, and follow through with writing your action steps. You owe it to yourself. Remember, living well is not a right – it's a choice.

Nourishing the Soul

Naomi Mallinson

Naomi Mallinson – perpetual student, professional dilettante, and perennial earth mother – has been cavorting on Planet Earth since June 10, 1945. After graduating with honors from Harvard University, she embarked on a lengthy and somewhat illustrious technical career in computer programming, systems analysis, and database design, with honorable mention duly appearing in Marquis *Who's Who of American Women.* Discontent with the heavily left-brained, highly structured orientation of her 9 to 5 corporate career adventures, she relieved boredom by moonlighting as a professional psychic on several national 900 lines, composing some keyboard music, and writing massive amounts of poetry in her spare time.

Still failing to find fulfillment, she ended her technical career in 1994, changed costumes, and re-emerged on the stage of life as a T-shirted Holistic Health Practitioner. While inventing and applying diverse forms of bodywork, she discovered that she had the ability to assist her clients in achieving transformational breakthroughs that enriched their lives. Problem: Only one person at a time fits on a massage table.

In 2000, Naomi turned to writing as a means to reach a broader audience and soon began publishing. She wrote the chapter Freeing the Heart in the book *Wise Women Speak: 20 Ways to Turn Stumbling Blocks into Stepping Stones.*

Naomi delivers an encouraging message to all who aspire to lives of true fulfillment: "It can be done! And here are a few tips on how."

Naomi Mallinson
Sandpiper Communications
PO Box 1801
La Mesa, CA 91944-1801
(619) 668-1060
surefooted1@earthlink.net
http://home.earthlink.net/~surefooted1

My Story

What happens to an utterly passionate soul when a cherished dream dies and a love relationship turns from a hearth flame to bitter ashes? For me, in February 2000, it was heartbreak and devastating depression. Over the course of many months of gloom, I found my body wasting away. Life force escaped from me inexorably, like sand running through my fingers. I struggled in vain to stem the tide of destruction. As time passed, my body became so debilitated that I could barely digest food.

Eating became a nightmare! No matter what I ate, it made me feel worse – more hungry instead of less, weaker instead of energized. Shopping, cooking, and eating became dreaded chores. Even though I selected, prepared, and ate the most wholesome foods imaginable, the meals set my body reeling. I spent the between-meal hours contending with bouts of extreme fatigue, heart palpitations, bowel distress, and severe mood swings.

The relentless process of emaciation marched on. I shrank from a slim 108-pound woman to a skin-and-bones 88-pound wreck. It wasn't fat that was vanishing, it was me. Muscle, tissue, and bone were melting away. Even my jawbone deteriorated, and my teeth began to loosen.

Finally, I started to notice that my dilemma wasn't just about food. Something deeper had to be going on. I felt that my soul itself was hungry, and crying out to be fed. Without the firm foundation of a satisfied soul, I had no context for nourishing my body.

How could I go about feeding my soul? In order to find out, I needed to get really still and allow my deepest feelings to surface. Every day I took some time to sit quietly and study my soul's appetite. I learned that, deep inside, I hungered for some very simple vittles. I longed to laugh. I wanted to play. I yearned to explore and try new things. My soul had a dire deficiency in fun, pleasure, and enjoyment. The remedy was simple enough, but it was a tall order for me. Steeped in despair, weary to the bone, and battling a continual barrage of bodily symptoms, I could hardly imagine the possibility of having a good time.

Grimly determined to start enjoying life, I set out to discover what might be fun for me. How about learning a new language? I had always enjoyed learning languages, and I felt curious about Hebrew. With its mysterious alphabet and unique linguistic structure, it intrigued my mind and aroused my curiosity. On a deeper level, Hebrew stirred my sense of roots and origins. Coming from a Jewish family, I had been shaped by the same culture, heritage, and history that gave rise to the Hebrew language.

Armed with a heap of books and tapes from the library, I dived into the daunting task of learning to read, write, and speak modern Hebrew. Progress was painfully slow. Nevertheless after several months I began to gain some fluency. One day, I encountered a woman at the grocery store who turned out to be from Israel. I immediately struck up a conversation with her in Hebrew as we stood side by side picking over the navel oranges. Amazingly, she could understand my halting utterances, and I could understand her replies. Instant bliss!

Continuing to study Hebrew, I branched out in my fun-generating activities. What about art? I had always enjoyed art as a child. I invested in some modeling clay, a box of crayons, and a variety of non-toxic paints, and experimented with all of them. Finger paints, water-colors, and poster paints especially turned me on, and painting soon became a favorite pastime.

As my spirits brightened, I became less obsessed with food, more relaxed about eating, and more flexible in my food choices. Some of my meals still brought on unwelcome symptoms, but now I could see the situation in a brighter light. Instead of despairing, I could simply say, "Whoops! That meal didn't work very well. Thank you, body, for letting me know I need to make some adjustments."

Little by little, I proceeded to heal. The endless aching in my heart – and stomach – gave way to a sense of satisfaction. What a delight to watch my body rebuild itself! I've regained stamina, healthy muscle tone, and the ability to digest a wide variety of foods. I'm especially thankful that my gums have become firm and healthy, giving me a good chance of retaining all my teeth.

Learning to nourish my soul has not only renewed my health and vitality. It has given me another significant gift as well. This gift is a new home, an internal one, just like the home I've always dreamed of living in. It's a peaceful and spacious place, with scenic natural surroundings. The picture windows let in lots of sunshine and fresh air and open onto gorgeous views. The garden abounds with colorful flowers, while the softly glowing hearth fire keeps me warm.

Nourishing the Soul

Have you ever trudged through an entire day? Every step takes lots of effort, as if you were climbing a steep hill. Once in a while you mutter, "Why bother?" but the force of habit or a vague sense of obligation keeps you plodding along.

Trudging happens when you lose contact with your own core of aliveness. Perhaps something in your circumstances has disturbed you, and you don't know how to deal with it. Unconsciously, you choose to numb out. Your body stiffens and tenses, shutting off feeling. You succeed in becoming oblivious to whatever anxiety, regret, or anger is churning inside of you, but the veil of oblivion smothers your feelings indiscriminately, even your innate enthusiasm for life.

In contrast, your favorite dreams and fondest memories have quite a different quality. They shine with genuine happiness and a gentle sense of ease. Rather than struggling and striving, you sail through the day with cheer and confidence, and your body shrugs off its habitual tension. Your clenched jaw, hunched shoulders, and stiff upper lip return to a pleasurably relaxed condition. Instead of trudging, you glide.

Deep, chronic hunger comes from the habit of moving stiffly through life, in opposition to the natural flow. Fulfillment comes from moving softly, in harmony with that flow.

Sleeping Soft

The scrub board becomes a lyre,
the dishpan rings out tunes of fire.

The magic runs in blood so red
the seeds of harmony are spread
before thee like the sand on wind.

So cast aside the emery board
and tend the fireside with an ear
to music sweeter and more dear
than baby's breath and sweet perfume
of love songs ended not too soon.

The mystery lies *between* the lines.
Look not too hard, but let it find
you sleeping soft
and raise you up aloft, aloft.

A fix-it manual for shriveled souls might consist of descriptions of various techniques – exercises you can perform in order to shift from trudging to gliding – but in order to be effective, techniques must rest on a firm foundation. Otherwise they can never bring you lasting results.

This foundation has to do with attitude and your fundamental approach to life. Do you wake up and greet the new day with a grumble or a smile? At the end of the day, do you fall asleep with a groan or a sigh of contentment?

In the sections that follow, I'll start out by giving you some guidelines on building a strong foundation. Then I'll describe some of my favorite techniques – recipes for meals that your soul can feast on!

Building a strong foundation

To live in a way that satisfies your soul, you need to reclaim the spontaneity you were originally born with, and loosen up whatever damaging constraints you've acquired in the course of your lifetime. Your success in this venture will depend on your ability to feel, honor, and express your own real nature in your day-to-day life.

For the best results, strive to cultivate the character traits that can support you. Character traits are your constant companions, so choose them wisely and well. Here are three of my favorites:

- Persistence
- Faith
- Celebration

Pay homage to persistence, make friends with faith, and lay out a welcome mat for celebration. They will become your staunchest allies.

Persistence

We live in an age of drive-through restaurants, "labor-saving" Caesarean births, and instant-winner lottery tickets. We're conditioned to seek quick fixes in every facet of life, even when it comes to the matter of nourishing the soul. We long for a Big Bang peak experience that will fly us over all the hurdles at once and deliver us into everlasting bliss.

Peak experiences and thundering bolts of insight do occur, but they're not enough all by themselves. Satisfying the soul's hunger takes place incrementally, one meal at a time. Who has ever become a master chef all at once? To gain mastery, garnish your culinary creations with plenty of persistence, patience, and practice.

Faith

Faith can be a scary word sometimes, as in the expression "blind faith." Yikes. With blind faith I might walk off the edge of a cliff like one of those cartoon characters who stroll out into midair and suddenly drop like a stone when they look down. That's not the kind of faith I'm talking about. I'm talking about a "seeing faith," a faith based on awareness.

At times when I've been sick and scared, I've often flailed about in a frantic search for knowledge. What's wrong? How can I fix it? What would help? One day, exhausted from a tense and lengthy research session, I paused to rest for a few minutes. In those moments of stillness, I overheard a whisper from somewhere inside me. It said, "Faith is more important than knowledge." I smiled and relaxed deeply, recognizing the truth of that statement.

With faith, knowledge will come, along with everything else that's necessary.

Celebration

My father often said, "*Carpe diem*: Seize the day!" To this sage advice I add, "Appreciate what is. Praise the day!"

When you set out to seize the day, you're devoting your energy to making the most of your opportunities and making your situation better. That's a useful approach, but it works even more successfully when you praise the day as well. Acknowledge and celebrate the goodness that's already present in your life. Your thankfulness and cheerful expectation will help you to recognize and gain from the opportunities that surround you.

Three strands of a braid

Persistence, faith, and celebration mutually support each other, like three strands in a braided rope. When persistence brings you great results, celebration naturally follows, and faith grows. All this happy celebrating will build your faith in life's goodness and spark your enthusiasm for persisting. Day by day, you'll forge a foundation you can truly count on.

Recipes: Hearty meals for the soul

Ready? Roll up your sleeves and tie on your apron. Here come three easy recipes you can use when your soul needs a nibble. In just a few minutes, you can whip up a warm and sinfully delicious, divinely satisfying treat. Savor it to your heart's content.

- Getting real
- Paying attention
- Kindling gladness

Getting real

By getting real, I mean getting real with yourself. To get real, simply acknowledge and express what you are actually feeling. No false fronts, smiling facades, or stiff stoicism. I usually notice the need to get real when I lose my enthusiasm and momentum, or find myself bogged down in glumness.

To get real, take time out from whatever you're busy doing. Notice where in your body you feel the most tension or discomfort, and if you can readily reach it, lay a hand there. Letting your awareness gently rest in that place, observe whatever sensations or images may come to you. Describe them out loud, making sure to mention what they remind you of. For example, "I feel cold and very scared, as if I'm standing outdoors in a gale wind and holding onto a flagpole for dear life." Submerged emotion will rise to the surface, allowing you to feel whatever turmoil you had been squelching.

Feel this turmoil fully and vividly, and express it spontaneously. You might laugh or cry or curse, or simply breathe out a sigh of compassion. Feeling and expressing your emotions will release them. Then you can resume your regular activities with a clear mind, an energized body, and a happy heart.

Paying attention

When distress gets you down, it's a sure bet that you've lost track of the present moment. You're either worrying about what might happen to you, or fretting over what has already taken place. Dwelling in the past or the future can hamstring you. Fortunately, it's not difficult to cut the strings. By paying attention to what's happening, you can promptly return to the here and now.

To pay attention, begin by noticing your breath. From moment to moment, what sensations do you feel as you breathe in and out? How is the rhythm of your breath? Which parts of your body are expanding and contracting?

Now deepen your present-moment focus by shifting your attention to your heartbeat. Hold a pulse point on your wrist or throat if that helps you tune in. Imagine you are listening to the drumming of your heart. Gently rock or sway to its music. What qualities do you notice? Does your heartbeat sound smooth or rough? Is it muted and soft or loud and emphatic?

Finally, focus your attention on whatever is presently happening. Notice all your sensory impressions, both internal and external. What do you observe in your environment? What sensations do you feel in your body?

Paying attention will calm you, restore your confidence, and set your feet squarely on the ground. Now you can take care of business with the focus and clarity it requires of you.

Kindling gladness

When your heart is heavy and your hearth is cold, it's time to rekindle the flame of gladness. Here's a reliable way to do just that. Speaking out loud in a firm voice, rattle off an extensive list of things you're glad about. Be sure to begin each announcement with feeling words. For starters, use low-key words such as "I'm glad . . ." or "I like . . ." You might say something like "I'm glad I can get fresh organic veggies at my local grocery store" or "I like how my dog comes to greet me when I get home at night."

After a dozen or so warm-up statements, you'll find your enthusiasm rising. At this point, switch to more emphatic opening phrases, such as "I love . . ." "I'm thrilled . . ." or "Hurray!" Make these pronouncements with gusto. You might declare, "I love the way my hair looks this morning!" "I'm thrilled that I got the perfect dress at 50% off!" or "Hurray! I've finished my tax return!"

By this time, you'll actually be feeling good. Continue to exclaim, proclaim, and rejoice for as long as you're having fun with it.

Naomi Mallinson

What's at the heart of happiness?

When you get in the habit of nourishing yourself, something lovely takes place. You don't have to "do it." It's a natural process that happens of its own accord. Your heart will open. It softens and gently unfolds, like the petals of a morning glory. When a situation comes along that startles you or feels threatening, your heart may hunker down for a while, but soon it will come out from hiding. More and more of the time, you'll bask in the glow of a happy, peaceful heart. It's this way of living that the soul thrives on. This is what feeds your deepest hunger.

To nourish your soul is simply to live as your natural self, fully and lusciously alive. Remember the story of Pinocchio? Imagine how he must have felt when he turned into a real live boy. No longer stiff and wooden, he could now stretch and walk and breathe. He could move about with strength and an easy grace. Nourishing the soul makes that kind of difference in your life.

You're here on this earth to dance, not to dangle from strings like a marionette. Feed your deepest hunger every day. Persist, have faith, and celebrate – especially at those times when celebrating is not easy. Take the time and make the effort. Your real life story will surpass the most ardent of your dreams.

Heart Open

A cigar store Indian? He stood
impassive,
made of wood.

Squaw handed him the baby girl.
Around his finger
hers did curl.

Heart open.

Squaw looked upon her husband tall.
"Sun shine.
Rain fall?"

He answered to his wife and daughter,
"Sun shine in, melt ice.
Warm water."

Get Out of Your Head
and Into Your Heart

Christine A. Moranetz, PhD

Christine Moranetz has evolved into a national leader in health promotion and disease prevention. She served as national President of the Association for Worksite Health Promotion, actively contributed to the development of the Health Fitness Director certification for the American College of Sports Medicine – being in the first 15 professionals to receive the certification – and served as an advisor/liaison to the Missouri Governor's Council on Physical Fitness and Health.

She served on the national board of the Association of Teachers of Preventive Medicine and was President of their Foundation. She currently serves on the Scientific Advisory Board for the Center for Living at Duke University.

A native of New Mexico, she completed most of her education in Oklahoma. A graduate of East Central University and Oklahoma State University, Christine moved to Kansas to pursue advanced studies at the University of Kansas and completed her PhD in Education: Exercise Physiology and Nutrition.

In her community, Christine served on the board of the AIDS Council of Greater Kansas City and recently joined the board of The

Coterie Theatre – a nationally acclaimed youth theater, where she is one of the founders and co-directors of the Dramatic AIDS Education Project.

Her health promotion expertise has grown over the years, having held the position of Manager of Lifewise Programs at St. Luke's Hospital of Kansas City, leading the program to national recognition. More recently, she serves as the manager of Women's Health Initiatives for Truman Medical Centers where she is contributing to initiatives that link research, education, and health promotion outreach programs with a faculty-based women's health care clinic.

She has held multiple academic positions, most recently, Clinical Associate Professor in the Department of Obstetrics and Gynecology in the School of Medicine, University of Missouri-Kansas City. She also holds Adjunct Associate Professor positions at the University of Kansas in the Department of Family Medicine in Kansas City and in the Department of Preventive Medicine in Wichita.

Christine is an accomplished public speaker and educator, with expertise in diverse topics related to lifestyle enhancement. She provides training for multiple national programs and corporations.

Christine A. Moranetz, PhD
Health Promotion Consultant
Prairie Village, Kansas
cmoranetz@yahoo.com

My Story

I'm an achiever. For as long as I can remember, I've been a doer and a leader. Saying "no" to people has always been hard. So, over commitment and "burning the candle at both ends" have been common in my life journey.

I started first grade when I was five and progressed through school – finishing high school at 16 and college at only 20. My achievements went beyond the classroom, as I became involved in multiple activities throughout high school and college.

While *doing* and *achieving* and *leading* can be great – these qualities also became negative aspects of my life. My parents, particularly my dad, placed great emphasis on making grades and performing well. While the intentions were good, and the goals admirable, I felt as if I was loved and appreciated only for what I did and what I achieved – not for who I was. It took a long time for me to sort out the "wrong reasons" for why I was achieving and to move on to a more productive and happy journey for my own reasons.

Not surprisingly, when my marriage was failing, I threw myself into my work. I harbored anger and pressed forward without dealing with the core reason for my unhappiness and discontent. It took some guidance – both professionally and from friends – to recognize that I could get out of my head and follow my heart. I have forgiven many who have hurt me and continue to forgive myself. I continue to achieve and accomplish many good things, but now I try to lead with my heart, honoring myself and others with love, appreciation, respect, and compassion.

One of the biggest growth experiences for me was forming a new relationship with my dad as a grown adult. During a difficult period when there was a lack of intimacy in my marriage, which began failing early in its 14 years, I found myself distant and cold with my colleagues and staff at work. Because my relationship wasn't good with my spouse, I channeled my energy into *doing* more – unfortunately, with a lot of negativity.

A great boss encouraged me to address the anger in my life. It came as a surprise that this emotion was what was under the surface of my pain and anguish. With professional counseling, I began to recognize that some of the underlying pain was still believing that I had to achieve for love and acceptance from dad and others – even at 30-something. Complicated by the pain of a failing marriage, I truly needed to actively address this distorted reason for living my life.

Through active counseling, participating in support groups, reading, journaling, and accepting encouragement from wonderful friends, I did some great healing work. It was during that period that I reinvented my relationship with "Daddy-o." To this day, I remember a letter I wrote him that shared my desire to embark on an adult relationship with him – that I was no longer his child, yet, always his daughter. I am pleased to say our relationship today is great.

My path has continued to bring my heart into my relationships. I had the pleasure of teaching health promotion and disease prevention to first-year medical students for over 10 years. I placed a priority on a well-being that went beyond the physical domain, into the mental, emotional, relational, and spiritual realms. And I began to be known as the professor who would hug them – an infrequent behavior in traditional medical school training.

My journey has brought me to a place where I'm letting down the walls that have prevented others from getting close to me. Having experienced rejection and lack of intimacy in my marriage, it was easier to just not get involved with anyone. Without even knowing, I set up boundaries that didn't let anyone get too close to me. After an amicable divorce, and many years of being on my own, I've come to accept, forgive, and love myself more. In doing so, I've opened up my world to more intimate relationships.

I view my life as a whole new journey in front of me. I live more in the now and try to enjoy every day with an attitude of appreciation. It is my hope that other women, regardless of their age or circumstances, can get in touch with their hearts and live their lives more fully. I have and it's made all the difference. As I truly celebrate entering mid-life, I'm happy to share an important part of my path and provide insight into how you can live more fully by getting out of your head and into your heart.

Get Out of Your Head and Into Your Heart

I had the remarkable experience a couple of years ago to participate in programs offered by Life Success, Inc.* What I went through was transformational – I was ready to live life through a different lens. One of the outcomes for me was to continue my life journey staying connected to who I really am and not to let achievement be the sole driver in my life.

---

* *Life Success Seminars, Inc.,* a nonprofit organization, 9248 Princeton Glendale Road, PO Box 1369, West Chester, OH 45071-1369, (513) 874-0555.

As a single professional woman, I have the demands of making a living, supporting a mortgage, and preparing for my retirement. Yet I also have learned to enjoy this journey with greater commitment, contentment, and compassion. I developed a mission for myself that transcends the physical being into the emotional, mental, relational, and spiritual. Let me share some of my path and recommend some stepping stones to a healthier you!

Desirable

- Address Your Self-Esteem

While I discovered that my self-esteem was tied into my achievements, I sought out ways to learn more about myself. There was professional counseling with psychologists, support groups with women also going through a divorce, and reading books that helped me to understand my family dynamics and the lack of intimacy in my marriage and other relationships.

Get at the core of your pain and learn why your self-value has been diminished. Seek out support and professional assistance. Don't be afraid to get clinical help with your depression and sadness.

- Learn from the Best and the Worst

My "best" boss helped me to see my pent-up anger, while my "worst" boss showed me his anger. I learned from both. While I've had people with compassion who have taught me through their examples, I've also had individuals teach me valuable lessons from their hostility and lack of professionalism. I struggled for years trying to get out of difficult relationships – both at home and at work. I had to recognize that I wasn't ready to move on and that I still had lessons to learn exactly where I was.

Be willing to learn from both the good and the bad examples of people in your life, particularly those in authority. Be patient with yourself and honor the timing of things in your life. Doors close for a reason – it's usually because there's a better door to open.

- Be Active and Eat Healthfully

Although physical activity and healthful eating have been at the core of my professional world, I had to find a personal plan that would work for me. Walking became the exercise of choice and diligently fitting it into my early morning routine was the most consistent path to improving my health. Walking – in silence – can be meditation in motion for me and this special time allows me to pray and sort through my feelings and emotions. As with many in pain, feeding my emotions with food or alcohol was common. I've had to change my attitude – and I no longer use either to dull the pain or squelch the fear.

Learn about your relationship with food and alcohol, and your attitude toward physical activity. Pursue how you can turn unhealthy patterns into ones that support your new path to wellness. Get a physical examination and use the results of ill health to motivate you to take better care of yourself.

Intimate

- Build Lasting Friendships

I've been so fortunate to have long-lasting friendships – most importantly, a group of women friends that I've known professionally – some for nearly 30 years. We named our group "WILD" – loosely standing for Women in Leadership Development. This group of WILD women has supported each other through many of life's sorrows – loss of a job, cancer, surgery, and the death of a spouse. Yet we're also there for each other to celebrate in life's joys – engagements, marriages, children's marriages, new jobs, and boyfriends.

Recognize the value of your friends and be there for them – they'll be there for you as well. Carve out time in your life to just be with them and to share in the mutual support and love that's so special.

- Forgive Yourself and Others

This practice can be transformational. I began to look at why someone who had hurt me behaved the way they did. I got the feelings of anger and frustration out by "writing them a letter" – no holds barred, cuss words intact – and never sent the letters. Then I wrote letters of forgiveness and understanding – some of these were sent, others were not. Yet releasing the feelings of anger and practicing forgiveness were many times the turning points of moving forward. As for forgiving myself, I began with recognizing that God has and will continue to forgive me and that has led me to become more compassionate and supportive of myself.

Find ways to feel the anger and express it in a healthy way. Whether it be journaling or beating a pillow – get it out! Then write out your feelings of forgiveness for yourself and others. When it's appropriate, share that forgiveness personally. Then, let it go and move on.

Courageous

- Try Something New

Little did I know that my regular Wednesday night dance classes would continue for over 12 years. I stumbled from being a newcomer to gliding across the dance floor doing the "quick step" with ease and grace in Pro-Am competitions, knowing that at any point a missed step could throw both me and my partner across the floor.

While I could have slipped intensely into the "achieving" mode, I always tried to focus on having fun and enjoying the thrill of it all. The most important life lesson, however, was that I didn't always have to be the leader. If I was going to win a competition, I had to follow and let someone else – my partner – be in charge. I came to know that if I stayed in my head and analyzed what I was doing, I never danced well. The time spent dancing has been some of the best work in helping me let go of fear and live life more joyfully.

Find a hobby; explore something that you've never done before that takes you out of your comfort zone. Make time to do something for yourself that allows you to develop beyond your work or family.

- Give to Others

On the other end of the spectrum, I learned that finding a way to give to others less fortunate gave me courage. I've had the pleasure of doing medical and health promotion ministry work with the people of Guatemala for the last three years. When I give to others who have so little, I see the immense courage they have just to live their lives. And by giving to others, I receive much more in return. To receive the unconditional love and appreciation from people when all you do is share a little of yourself is exhilarating.

Find a way to get out of your own world and give to others less fortunate. Work a soup kitchen, mentor a child in her reading, volunteer at a homeless or domestic violence shelter. Even if you don't have the financial resources to give to others, your time and talent shared with others who are in conditions far more difficult than your own can help you overcome your fears and learn from their courage.

- Avoid Avoidance

Procrastination and avoidance are persistent patterns in my life – driven by the fear of failure and my desire to be perfect. I have truly mastered putting off the most difficult of tasks and avoiding conflict with others. I'm learning to let go of the perfectionism and as Nike would say – *Just do it!*

I've found that jumping in to tackle the most difficult of tasks first is a successful strategy. The feeling of accomplishment is profound, and then it takes minimal energy to do the easier tasks. As for avoiding conflict, I've found that my perception of how big the issue is – is far bigger than reality. A healthy way of relating to others in difficult circumstances is for me to approach them with how "I feel," rather than judging them. The sense of relief that comes from being upfront with someone is so much better than bottling up the emotions.

Become aware of the ways in which you let fear get in the way of completing difficult tasks or communicating directly with others. Ask others to give you feedback and to support you when you need help.

Peaceful

- Gratitude Journal

Thanks to Sarah Ban Breathnach in her book, *Simple Abundance,* and the encouragement of Oprah Winfrey in her regular talk show – I started to do frequent writing in a gratitude journal. Different from other journaling I do, I reflect on all the things for which I'm thankful. I've come to recognize that I'm not only grateful for the obvious "things" I have – my home, my job, my financial security – but I'm also deeply grateful for my family and friends.

Start a journal and a ritual for writing down your thoughts. By writing in the early morning, you can start your day with a positive attitude. By logging before you go to bed, you can let go of the day's anxieties and enjoy a more peaceful slumber.

- Be Silent - Pray and Meditate

Just as with the gratitude journal, I've made a conscious effort to pray. While I've relied on the common prayers of the rosary from my Catholic upbringing, I've also tried to just be silent. That means turning off the TV and the radio – usually put on to drown out the silence of isolation and pain. Being still – and letting God flow into my heart also helps me let go of anxieties and the jumbled to-do list in my head. I also listen to a meditative tape before I go to work, which helps me focus and enter the day with clarity and peacefulness.

Find a way to be still and quiet. Learn meditative techniques, such as deep breathing. Participate in yoga. Make this time for yourself a priority.

- Live in the Now

A lot of my life has been spent regretting things from the past and worrying about the future. It's not surprising that I've suffered from chronic tension headaches ever since my college years. I have rarely lived fully present in the moment. By taking one day at a time, I'm learning to focus on whatever is happening around me.

I've come to recognize that there are no coincidences. People and events come into my life for a reason. A friend recommended that I read Eckhart Tolle's *The Power of Now*. I've found that his guide to spiritual enlightenment has helped me be a more loving human whose focus is shifting to my relationships and away from achieving and doing.

Be aware of the little things that happen around you every day. The people who come into your life are there, as the saying goes – for a reason, a season, or a lifetime. Celebrate each moment with loving appreciation.

—— ◆ ——

While I'm attempting to live my life with greater ease and appreciation, I'm pleased to say that I'm happier now than I have ever been in my life. I still haven't mastered the techniques that I've described, but practicing and integrating them into my life has become a priority. It's not to say that I still don't have issues to deal with, relationships to heal, challenges to confront, or decisions to make. It's just that I strive daily to remember that my "heart-filled" journey will be easier, more loving, and blessed than if I stayed only in my head.

My name is Christine Ann Moranetz – and I am a Desirable, Intimate, Courageous, and Peaceful Woman!

One Foot in Yesterday and the Other in Tomorrow: What about Today?

Kim Lyons-Weiland,
RN, BSN, LBSW, IBCLC, CM

As the Director of Women's Health Services at the Buena Vista Regional Medical Center in Storm Lake, Iowa, Kim Lyons-Weiland was at the height of her career in October 2001 when she was diagnosed with breast cancer. Facing a bilateral mastectomy and chemotherapy, she knew her life would be changed forever.

Over the next six months, Kim learned the importance of living in the here and now. "When I finally faced my cancer head on, and allowed myself to experience all that went with it," she recalls, "I realized I was on the journey of a lifetime, and I wanted to be there."

Following her recovery, Kim joined the staff at Sports Rehab & Professional Therapy Associates where she currently manages their newest service line, Uniquely You. Drawing from her personal experience and expertise in women's health, she developed and implemented Uniquely You to meet the needs of women who have undergone, or who are preparing to undergo, breast surgery. With her trademark compassion and professional expertise, Kim fits women for post-mastectomy prostheses, while offering support, encouragement, and a message of hope.

Named Citizen of the Year in 1994 and again in 2001 by the *Storm Lake Pilot Tribune*, for her personal and professional contributions to Storm Lake and the surrounding community, Kim was also named Honorary Chairperson for the area's 2002 Relay For Life. In addition to serving on numerous boards and committees, Kim is credited with implementing Maternal/Newborn Case Management and Lactation Consultant Services within Buena Vista County. She has worked extensively with pregnant and parenting teens in area school systems and is co-founder of PROP (Parents Reaching Out to Parents).

With her characteristic enthusiasm and humor, Kim continues to do speaking engagements and professional consultation in the area of women's health. A graduate of Briar Cliff College, Kim is a registered nurse and licensed social worker. Previously certified in Childbirth Education and Inpatient Obstetrics, she continues to maintain her board certification as a Lactation Consultant and was recently Certified as a Mastectomy Fitter.

The mother of four sons, Kim and her husband, Tony, live in Alta, Iowa.

Kim Lyons-Weiland, RN, BSN, LBSW, IBCLC, CM
Uniquely You/ Sports Rehab & Professional Therapy Associates
315 West 5th
Storm Lake, IA 50588
(712) 732-7724
(712) 213-1072 fax
kimweiland@yahoo.com

My Story

Cancer. The word itself evokes fear. We hear it everyday, "Did you hear about so and so? She has cancer." Or "Isn't it sad about so and so having cancer, she is so young!" I've heard it and I've said it, all the while thanking God that I wasn't the recipient of the dreaded diagnosis. Yet, deep down inside, I knew that someday I wouldn't be able to dodge that cancer bullet. My father hadn't, my sister hadn't, and in October 2001, I hadn't either.

In my junior year of high school I got the call from my sister. My father had been diagnosed with skin cancer and wasn't expected to live. At 17, it was hard for me to grasp the reality of his illness, not to mention his impending death. My parents had divorced six years earlier, and I hadn't seen my dad in almost four years. I tried to comfort my sister as she cried at the other end of the phone. I felt totally helpless. Our father died three months later.

It was a difficult time, particularly for my two older sisters. His wife wouldn't allow us to have any contact with him during his illness and requested that we not attend his funeral. I can remember reading the obituary: Jack had three stepchildren, Larry, Moe, and Curly [the actual names escape me] and three daughters by a previous marriage. It was the first time I remember turning my anger into action. Instead of pouting, ranting, and raving, I promptly called the editor of the paper. Using the most adult voice I could muster, I informed him that there had been an unfortunate misprint. He apologized and graciously offered to reprint a corrected obituary, which my sisters and I took great pleasure in reading the following day.

Strike two

It wasn't until 1996 that I would face my second encounter with cancer. It was a beautiful March afternoon when I heard the phone ring from the driveway. I got there just in time to catch the call with a breathless, "Hello?" I thought I heard my sister's voice, but wasn't sure.

"Jan, is that you?" It sounded like she was crying, "What's wrong? Are you OK?" I asked.

"I . . . have . . . cancer. The doctors said I have . . . leukemia," she said through her tears.

"What? Are you sure?" I asked, not waiting for a response. "I'm coming Jan, don't worry, I'll be there as soon as I can!"

Jan was the middle sister, I was four years younger. She hadn't had it easy growing up, but, at 43, she was happily married to a great guy and had two beautiful children. No one deserved that happiness more than Jan. Growing up, she was one of the few constants in my life. She was my rock when I needed her, my level-headed, logical, sound-advice-giving big sister. I loved her and I couldn't lose her. This had to be a misdiagnosis.

Following a year and a half of treatment that showed little progress, Jan decided to get a second opinion. It revealed that she had non-Hodgkin's lymphoma, not leukemia. The news was bittersweet because she now had another option, but had lost precious time.

Jan had decided to undergo a bone marrow transplant if a donor could be found. My sister and I were both tested in hopes of being potential donors. I can still hear her voice the day I got the call, "We're a perfect match!" She giggled at the other end of the phone. I was ecstatic. I was going to be the donor for Jan's bone marrow transplant, and she was going to be just fine. Thank you, God!

It was April 17, 1998. I was packing for a conference in Des Moines when the phone rang. It was my sister Debby. She called to tell me that Jan was being admitted to the hospital for shortness of breath. I could hear the concern in her voice. I told her I would come down there that night to check things out and go to my conference from there on Friday. I could hear the relief in her voice.

I left home around 4:30 that afternoon with my 17-year-old son, Adam, who had graciously offered to give up his weekend to make the trip with me. We pulled into the hospital parking lot around 10:00 p.m. As we entered the lobby, I saw my brother-in-law walking rapidly toward the door, "If you want to see your sister, you better get up there now!"

My heart was in my throat as I ran to the elevator. Please, God, please let her be OK, I kept praying. I ran down the hall until I reached the double doors that opened to the intensive care unit. As I entered, I saw my sister Debby, Jan's husband, and my two nieces and my nephew walking toward me. Instinctively I knew that Jan was gone. I remember throwing my purse in the corner screaming, "No! Get away from me!" It was as if I was watching myself, I felt totally disconnected. It was all a muffled blur.

"It's OK, mom, it's OK," Adam whispered softly through his tears as he held me in his arms. Time stood still.

Strike three

I was, at what some would consider, the height of my professional career on Sept. 24, 2001. Being sought out to fill the position of director for the soon-to-be-built women's center was not only flattering, it was a position I had dreamed of. In addition to directorship, I would also sit on the hospital's administrative team. Life couldn't get much better than this.

As the end of my first year approached, architectural plans were nearing completion, program development was under way, and I was actively communicating to the public the vision for the women's center. By all outward appearances, I was enthusiastically fulfilling my role as the Director of Women's Health Services. But outward appearances and reality were as different as night and day.

I was exhausted and overwhelmed both physically and emotionally. I was working close to 60 hours a week as a one-woman department, and I found myself walking a fine ethical line, for the sake of political correctness. I was losing sleep, working late, and had started isolating myself from my family – everything was about work. I found myself slipping back into the old familiar patterns of workaholism that I thought I had tackled long ago. I knew I couldn't do this much longer, something had to change, and it did. I was diagnosed with breast cancer.

I found the lump while in the shower doing a routine breast self-exam. I rationalized it as probably being a hormonal cyst, although I knew it was unlike anything I had ever felt before. The next day I decided to see my doctor; he recommended an ultrasound. I scheduled it for the following day.

Lying on the ultrasound table, I could see the screen, as the radiology tech went over the lump. I'm no radiologist, but as I studied the screen, I knew that this was not a cyst, it was a solid mass. By that afternoon, I was in Sioux City seeing Dr. Qalboni at the Breast Center. Following a mammogram, an ultrasound, and a fine-needle aspiration, I was on my way home. I would have the results on Monday.

Monday started like any other day: administrative team meeting, phone calls, business as usual. After spending my lunch hour with a supportive friend, I headed home to receive my anticipated call.

"Hello? Yes, yes, I understand. Yes, I will. Thanks so much for calling," I heard myself say.

I felt a cold trickle run down my chest, landing on my breast – it was a tear. It was than I realized I was crying. I had breast cancer. For the second time in my life, time stood still.

Opening the door of inner strength

It hit me from behind like an ocean wave, knocking me down, leaving only the burn of salt water in my nostrils and throat. Sputtering and coughing, I struggled to stand up, only to be knocked down again and again. I laid my head on the kitchen table and cried. The emotions were overpowering. Fear, anger, panic, guilt! A thousand thoughts raced through my head in a split second. What was I going to do? God, please help me.

It was then that I realized that I had a choice to make. I could start swimming with the waves and make it to shore, or I could keep getting knocked down, unable to do anything but sputter and cough. I decided I wanted to swim, and believe it or not, breast cancer became my lifeline. Suddenly my fear of professional failure was gone – replaced with an overwhelming desire to live.

We all ride the roller coaster of adversity during our life, facing unexpected trials and challenges. Although my seat may be different, the rides I've taken are really no different than yours. We take off white knuckled, hanging on for dear life, laughing one minute and terrified the next. Taking that whipping turn just in the nick of time, only to find ourselves flying down a slope at a speed we're certain will throw us from the track.

Yes, my experiences with cancer were crazy rides, but believe it or not, they were rides that have turned into multiple blessings. Cancer didn't throw me from the track; it (eventually) put me on the right track. It became a key that opened a door of inner strength I didn't realize I had.

You've had challenges that have taken you on crazy rides. It doesn't have to be cancer, believe me, cancer is *not* the trial of all trials, there are far worse things. For example, living your entire life with a dream or desire that you never pursue. Or making the destination of your dream more important than the journey that is taking you there.

Destinations can change, I am living proof of that, but the journey is our day-to-day reality, it's our here and now.

I made it through the loss of my breasts, the chemotherapy, even being bald, but what I saw as almost a greater challenge was still ahead of me. I knew what I needed to do to stay alive, and it involved more than nutrition and exercise. I needed to leave my position as the Director of Women's Health Services. The fear of losing my place on the career ladder, and all that I had worked so hard for, had melted away. It was a decision that would change the course of my professional path. A decision that, as some of my colleagues put it, would be "professional suicide." After being back at work for three weeks, I turned in my letter of resignation.

Would I have been able to make that decision had I not faced the challenge of breast cancer? I don't think so. Cancer threatened my very existence. In an instant, living became my passion and survival my goal. My destination had changed without warning. Had I wasted the journey I had traveled thus far? Of course not! I believe now more than ever that nothing in life happens by chance, but that we are guided instead by a divine plan, put in place for our ultimate good. The lessons we learn in this life are never wasted, just as the walk through adversity is never without meaning.

One Foot in Yesterday and the Other in Tomorrow: What about Today?

Determine where you are

I thought I knew where I was. Remember? I was on the career path of a lifetime – somewhere I had always dreamed of being. Or was I? If everything was so great, then why was I so miserable? Because I was so busy catching up from yesterday and worrying about tomorrow, I was never living in today. It was only when I heard those words, "I'm sorry Kim, the biopsy showed malignant cells," that I became acutely aware of where I was, and you know what? It wasn't where I wanted to be.

If you want to make a significant change in your life, you must determine where you are right now. I encourage you to take 10 or 15 minutes and find a quiet place with no distractions, where you can sit and consciously focus on you. Then pick one area of your life, be it work, family, spirituality, whatever you prefer, and determine where you are right now. Then ask yourself: Are you an active participant, or are you just going through the motions? Are you semi-conscious, with too many irons in the fire? Are you living in the here and now, or do you have one foot in yesterday and one foot in tomorrow?

Consider the impact that not living in the moment can have on your life. You will never realize your desire, your dream, or God's will for your life with one foot in yesterday and one foot in tomorrow. Take it from a pro. I have straddled more todays than you can imagine. Remember, the destination can change without a moment's notice.

Recognize and redirect

If you were on a trip and realized by looking at your map that you were going north, but your desired destination was northeast, would you change your direction? Of course you would! Life is a journey, as well. Are you going in the right direction? You've recognized, I hope, where you are in a specific area of your life. Now it's time to ask yourself, am I on course? If you are, that's great. If you're not, be honest with yourself and admit it, and consider changing your direction.

Let's take it a little further. You've changed your direction, and according to the map, you're back on course. But as you travel your journey, you happen to stop in the most awesome place. In fact, you like it much better than the original destination you had planned for. Hmm . . . do you change your plans? But you've been planning this trip for so long, how will you explain such a drastic change in plans? Does the destination or dream you desire satisfy your expectations? Re-evaluate your desired destination, as well as the road that is leading you in that direction. You may decide to redirect.

How? Have you had to navigate any sudden twists and turns, unexpected bumps or potholes along your journey's path? Of course you have. If you hadn't, you'd have left this planet long ago. Making it through that terrain equipped you with a tool you may not even realize you have, the ability to redirect. You've swerved to the right to avoid that pothole; you took a sharp left to make that unexpected curve. It may be a strength that's buried somewhere deep inside, but you have it, so start digging.

Around and over the mountain

I once heard a pastor tell the story of Moses and the Israelites' journey out of Egypt, into the Promised Land, in such a way that it had a profound impact on me. I specifically remember him telling how a trip that should have taken days took 40 years. Why? Because it took more than one trip around the mountain for the Israelites to learn the valuable lessons the Lord was trying to teach them. Lessons that were essential to their survival. So around and around they went for 40 years. I assure you that the sermon I heard was much more theologically sound, but you get the message.

How many times do you plan to go around that same mountain before you recognize and embrace the lessons laid out before you? Those lessons are the tools that become your strategies for getting from where you are to where you want to be.

We tend to think of mountains as our challenges, our trials, our certain adversity in life, but they can also be the peaks from which we see the forest for the trees. Trust me, you can see so much more from that summit than you will ever see looking up at that cliff.

I believe with all of my heart that nothing in this world happens by chance, but instead as the result of a divine plan, with a divine purpose in mind. Following my recovery, I joined the staff at Sports Rehab & Professional Therapy Associates in Storm Lake, Iowa. Drawing from my personal experience with cancer and expertise in the area of women's health, I implemented Uniquely You, a service designed to meet the needs of women who have undergone, or are preparing for, breast surgery.

By the grace of God I was given the courage to redirect, resulting in making a career change that I would have never thought possible. Only He could take the devastation of breast cancer and turn it into such a blessing. I can now stand on the summit of that mountain and see all the possibilities that lie ahead. I am on the journey of a lifetime, and I plan to stay in today and enjoy the ride.

Teaching What You Need to Learn –
Finding Your True Path

Barbara Bernadette

Barbara Bernadette is a self-made woman who expects the most out of life. For 27 years she has been an entrepreneur. Barbara is the founder of The Healing Money Program, an Enrolled Agent with the Internal Revenue Service, and a business and financial coach. She describes herself as a money alchemist because she teaches people how to turn their debts into gold.

At age 54, Barbara believes she is just starting out on the life she was meant to lead.

In 2002 she sold her tax practice in California's Napa Valley and bought a farm in Oregon. She says she was born to empower people through her writing, speaking, and teaching. The move to Oregon and the farm have created the space for her to fully embrace this path.

Barbara pioneered The Healing Money Program, an innovative set of tools and principles that create a healthy and wealthy relationship with money, as a natural extension of her financial and teaching background. She brings an intuitive spiritual presence to individuals and groups who are seeking solutions to money and life issues.

As a mentor, financial and business coach, workshop leader, and keynote speaker, Barbara's message is powerful. She offers a new outlook on how to integrate career, financial, and personal goals into a healthy and balanced lifestyle.

Barbara Bernadette
The Healing Money Program
(541) 607-6569 Oregon, USA
(707) 963-8307 California, USA
www.healingmoney.com
info@healingmoney.com

My Story

When I was 8 years old, sitting on the back of my father's vegetable truck, I heard Spirit giving me direction. At that time, all I knew for sure was that my life was about teaching and empowering people. I also knew learning and writing would hold a significant place in my life. With the founding of my Healing Money Program, these childhood "knowings" were put into form.

I founded The Healing Money Program out of a natural progression of changing my own life into one of abundance, growth, and healing. In 1988 I went through a divorce. At that time my sons were 5 and 10, and I was making $600 a month. My house payment was also $600 a month, and my day care bill was $500 a month. I was a self-employed part-time bookkeeper. Within a year I bought my ex-husband out of our home, paying him $35,000. I now own the farm, a beautiful Victorian home in the heart of the Napa Valley, and a rental. All of my accomplishments have been achieved by using the tools of my Healing Money Program.

To change my life, I started listening to Spirit. I asked Spirit to supply what I wanted and needed: more clients, steady income, and a life that held meaning. I went back to school and became an Enrolled Agent, expanding my work into a full-service tax practice. It was through my spiritual work that I discovered the art of manifesting my dreams and making them a reality. I learned that our thoughts create our beliefs and actions. I realized all work is internal work, that the outer world is simply a reflection of our personal, internal world.

I discovered how powerful we are as individuals and how scared we are of acknowledging our power. To truly come into my own personal power, I needed to go through a transformation of healing, of learning that I truly deserved all the abundance Spirit says is rightfully mine. As my own life changed and I became more abundant financially, spiritually, and in relationships, my clients started asking me to teach them how to change their own lives. I always knew I was born to teach. In fact, I graduated from San Jose State University with a teaching credential. Now I had before me the opportunity to truly create a program that combined all of my loves, gifts, and talents.

The Healing Money Program concentrates on the emotional and psychological relationship we have with our money. I believe our financial condition is merely an outer reflection of our internal belief system of what we truly deserve in life. Once we can heal our lives internally, we will allow our financial well being to show up. These are the eight elements of The Healing Money Program:

- Understanding
- Growth
- Manifesting
- Attracting
- Healing
- Forgiveness
- Encouragement
- Creativity

The program is delivered through keynote speeches, lectures, workshops, corporate coaching, individual coaching, and card readings. An essential element – the Healing Money Cards – incorporate all eight program elements and are used as a tool for understanding the concepts of the program and each individual's personal money issues.

For true success and fulfillment each day, followers must practice the eight elements of the program. For me, staying on course means I must practice what I preach and learn what I teach.

Teaching What You Need to Learn –
Finding Your True Path

You were born with a dream and a calling

Stepping stones solidify into pathways in many different ways. For me, buying a farm was the final transformation. I bought the farm to truly concentrate on my writing and getting my message out into the world. It is time to harvest my creativity, to grow and produce the fruits of all my labors, and to turn my ideas, dreams, and talents into my mission and gift to the world. It is here that my calling is screaming to be heard. I can no longer play small at what I do. The time has arrived. I sit here and write.

I ask you to ponder these questions:

- Who are you to play small?
- Who are you to not stand up and own the power that you are?
- Who are you to stay home in Kansas and never find the yellow brick road?
- Who are you to not drag out the bags of sand and transform your stepping stones into your own unique pathway?

I'm asking you to find the courage to begin. I will share with you what I am doing as a guidepost, as a light, as a source of inspiration to help you on your way. That is a main piece of my work: lighting the way for others. Showing how it can be done. Leading by example.

As you go through this process of transformation with me, I ask you to remember these five messages:

1. Remember who you are.
2. Remember why you must do this.
3. Seek support.
4. Voice your fears.
5. Have others voice your beliefs for you when you are so scared or so stuck you can't do it for yourself.

Sleep: Most of us believe we have something special to offer the world. Somewhere deep inside we believe it. But usually we are too afraid to voice it, to acknowledge it, or to bring it out in the open. We think we will look conceited or stupid if we voice our inner truth. We are also afraid it will not meet with approval by those we love.

If you own your "specialness," it probably means something in your life will have to change. Perhaps your loved ones will tell you that you are crazy. Maybe you will quit the job you have always hated. Perhaps you won't be able to live in the same house, town, or state anymore. Acknowledging who you are on a deeper level will trigger change. It will ignite a fire. It will make you breathe in a new way. All of this means you will no longer be who you have been up until this point.

So you sleep. You keep these ideas, this creativity, these special gifts that you possess deep within your unconscious. You sleep. Sometimes you drowse, almost wake up. But more often than not you just change position and keep sleeping. I am asking you to wake up. I am asking you to remember who you were born to be. I am asking you to forge into life and find the courage to create all the magnificence you can in the world. I am asking you to remember.

Remembering: Stepping stones are the groundwork or foundation of the structure called your path. Stepping stones arrive as bumps in that road, as stumbling blocks. They are hard times. They are the seeds that appear in your life as lessons, giving you the opportunity to flower and blossom, giving your life fullness and meaning. When you turn hard experiences, stumbling blocks, into bits of wisdom that build character, you create stepping stones.

My first son was born deaf. His deafness was at first a stumbling block but quickly became a huge stepping stone for me. Because of his disability, my life changed dramatically. His deafness gave me the stepping stones of strength, compassion, and the will to fight for what I believed in. Being his mother has never been easy, but the growth it has given me is phenomenal. I know sign language and communicate with the deaf. I am a bridge between the hearing world and the deaf world. My favorite heroine as a child was Helen Keller. Little did I know how closely I would relate to her world.

Being a single mother and raising two sons was also a stepping stone. It was challenging. I can remember the year my youngest was in the eighth grade and my oldest was a senior in high school. This was a hard time, because they did not have a strong male figure in their lives. I remember thinking, "This is probably as hard as it gets." Now they are both incredible young men and fathers. They are truly what I love most in the world, my biggest accomplishment.

Being a self-employed entrepreneur was another stepping stone. It is not for the light hearted. Not having a guaranteed income, a benefit package, or a retirement fund means you must truly believe in yourself and your ability to make a living and support your family. You must be a risk taker and have an incredible sense of "I can do this" or you won't make it. Tenacity is key to succeeding.

The development of my Healing Money Program is my cornerstone and has truly been the sand that has turned my stepping stones into a pathway. My program incorporates my business expertise, the importance of healing our lives, developing a healthy relationship with money, and understanding abundance is ours by divine right. Motherhood, deafness, and being an entrepreneur have created my own divine path. None of it has been easy, but all of it has given my life meaning.

Find your own way

Signposts: Look at your own life. Remember what it is you feel you must do to make your life have meaning. If you don't know what that is, go to that place deep inside of you and listen to the call of Spirit. Hear the voice that speaks with wisdom, the voice of inner knowing. The quieter you become, the more you pay attention to it, the louder it will sound. As you listen, become aware of the stepping stones in your life. Write them down. See how they create a pathway.

Voices: Understand and recognize the difference between the voice of Spirit and the voice of the ego. Pay attention to what you know is the right step, the right movement, the right choice. Practicing discernment is key in staying on your path. Learn who is speaking and guiding you. It is important to know which voice you are listening to. These two voices are very different.

- *Spirit*: When you start on your path, it is Spirit calling you to your work. It first plants seeds, creates the stepping stones. It guides you to follow your dreams and inner calling. Staying in alignment means you keep hearing the voice of Spirit. Spirit will whisper, "Here, let me guide you, follow me, learn from what is in front of you."

- *Ego*: The ego kicks in once you believe you are an authority in your area of expertise. It wants you to forget about the reason you have formed your path in the first place. The ego lives for the present moment, not for the deeper meaning of life. It will tell you, "Do what I say. Don't worry about practicing what you preach. You are now the authority. Forget having to do the work. You've already accomplished it!" The ego does not care about integrity or authenticity.

Sometimes we forget the reasons we started on our path in the first place. When we listen to the voice of ego more than that of Spirit, our lives can go awry. Jonathan and Ted illustrate this point.

- Jonathan is a cardiovascular surgeon who loves his work and his family but spends most of his time in the operating room. To stay healthy, he is taking dietary supplements. His own children eat mostly junk food because of his hectic lifestyle. Although he is the cardiovascular expert, he is putting his own children at risk for heart disease. Doesn't he realize they may end up on his operating table one day?
- Ted is a financial planner who can't wait to tell everyone about how much money he manages for his clients. He is very impressed with his accomplishments and his own income. Even though his income is in six figures, he has run up extreme amounts of credit card debt. He has also ruined his ex-wife's credit by taking out credit cards in both their names. Ted has lost sight of handling his own money in a conscientious, sound way and is undermining his own financial future. Is this the kind of advisor you would want managing your money? He is obviously not following his own financial advice.

Ego traps: Once our path has had its foundation laid and we have traversed it several times, we become the authority in our field. Once we become the authority, the ego kicks in and we may become lax. Next we feel we no longer need to practice what we preach. We have succeeded at this already, now our job is to instruct others in what we have learned ourselves. We become outer directed, being paid to tell others how to do it correctly. We become the cobbler whose children now go without shoes. We first made shoes for our family out of necessity; now we do it for money and recognition.

Teach what you need to learn

Being tested: Because our true path comes from the guidance of Spirit, we truly don't know all Spirit has in store for us to learn. This is the reason we **teach what we need to learn.**   Our path lies somewhere between the magical yellow brick road to Oz and the towering strength of the Great Wall of China. The promise is not to have an easier life, but a more profound one, as shown in these three examples. Depth and meaning are key words.   Our life becomes more profound, much bigger and deeper, more full of meaning, when we are forced to face our own dragons on a personal level and keep on doing the work we are here to do.

- Daniel, a brilliant, happily married heart surgeon, looked forward to being a father. After his wife had several miscarriages, their child was finally born. Daniel helped in the delivery, only to discover that his skills as a heart surgeon could not save his newborn son. The child was born with a heart abnormality and lived in his father's arms for only 20 minutes. All of his skills as a heart surgeon could not save his only child.
- Lindsey is a special education teacher for the severely retarded. She married and had her first child. As soon as Jason was born, it was apparent Lindsey's path would be changed forever. He was born a severe Downs syndrome child and will never be able to function on his own.
- Paula has a brilliant career as an authority on how the brain works. She travels worldwide giving lectures on the brain. Three years into her work her husband developed a brain tumor and faced a long difficult death.

All of these lives seem full of irony. All three experts in their fields were helpless in saving or changing the fates of those who meant the most to them.

I am not responsible for making you believe it.
My responsibility is to tell you about it.
St. Bernadette of Lourdes

The importance of integrity

Bernadette Soubirous of Lourdes, France, was only 14 when she witnessed the first of her 18 visions of the Virgin Mary in 1858. At that time she had no idea she would impact the lives of so many people. Today the cathedral at Lourdes is the second most visited place in France. More than five million visitors a year from over 150 countries come to drink and bathe in its holy, healing water. Bernadette's mission was to believe in the visions she saw. Her path was to tell about the miracles of the Virgin Mary. Even though the church at first condemned her, she stayed committed to what she knew was true. She was clear about her purpose. Eventually the church made her a saint.

Maria Smith was one of two policewomen who died in the south tower of the World Trade Center on Sept. 11, 2001. Using her flashlight she led people out of the building, telling them not to look. She was their light. She told them not to look because what she saw around her were body parts and horror. Her mission was to guide them to safety. She died not only a heroine but true to her path. She walked the walk, talked the talk. Her authenticity and integrity were deeply interwoven with her spirit.

A saint and a heroine. Most of us fall somewhere between the two. What both of them teach us is the importance of integrity and authenticity. Can you be as strong as Bernadette, as brave as Maria? Can you live authentically and with integrity? Both of these elements are key to living on purpose.

Voice your fears: Because you are human there will be times you want to quit, change course, or throw in the towel. This is when you must be sure you voice your fears. Living with integrity means going back to the focus of your work. Get grounded again. When you get off course, when you feel you are slipping off the edge, call for help. Surround yourself with people who support you. Have them remind you what you stand for. This is again the time you must remember *you are learning what you teach.*

Not only to teach, but to practice

Stay on your path with your vision before you and practice your own expertise over and over again. Go back to yourself. Look at what you are teaching. Do your own program over and over again. Are you a financial person? Practice about money. Are you in the health field? Practice good health. Are you a teacher? Teach yourself. Are you in marketing? Market yourself. It's why you are here. Not to give a message, but to practice a message.

If you want to make a difference in the world, if you want your life to have an impact on others, practice what you preach. **People learn not by what they are told, but by what they observe.** Live with integrity. Be the cobbler who makes shoes for her children.

Steps for Embarking on Your Path

1. Write down a desire from childhood.
2. List the stepping stones that have appeared in your life.
3. How does your childhood desire fit in with your stepping stones?
4. Write down three statements made by Spirit. See how they fit in with being on your path.
5. List three statements that come from the ego. See how they do not serve you.
6. Remember to stay in integrity.

The Imposter Syndrome

Fern Carness, MPH, RN

Fern Carness, MPH, RN, is a registered nurse with a background in critical care. Known as a Voice for Women's health, Fern travels extensively speaking to women's groups about their health status and how to become empowered to partner with the health care system.

An entrepreneur at heart, Fern has founded four successful health care-related businesses. Invasive Diagnostic Specialists, a cardiac catheterization lab staff relief service, provides high-caliber nurses to work in the area of invasive cardiology. This company was one of the first to recognize that nurses could work as independent contractors, bill fee-for-service, and function as businesswomen.

Frustrated with the lack of health promotion in the hospital setting, Fern founded Wellness At Work, Inc., in 1986 – a worksite health promotion company dedicated to improving the health status of individuals, one person at a time. For 10 years, Fern reached thousands with her health promotion messages, and then sold the company to Times Mirror, and became Principal at Carness Health Management, LLC.

Her new company created many health behavior change programs in print, video, audio, and Web formats, including Ready Set

STOP! a smoking cessation self-help program and A Wise Woman's Approach to Healing and Cancer. Currently, Fern is the co-owner of Just Like a Woman, a retail experience that blends specialty lingerie needs with health education and survivor support services in a feminine environment. Here women with medical challenges find the products they need while being treated with dignity and kindness.

Whether sewing Halloween costumes, making heirloom quilts, trekking in the Himalayas, or dragon boating on the Willamette, Fern never sits still. While crewing a dragon boat, Fern and her breast cancer survivor teammates, known as Pink Phoenix, rescued a suicidal man who had jumped off a bridge. They were awarded the Medal of Valor from the City of Portland. Fern is a gold medal paddler who represented the United States Senior Women at the 4th World Dragon Boat Championships in August 2001 in Philadelphia.

Fern lives in Portland, Oregon, with her husband of over 34 years. Fern and Al have two sons and two beautiful granddaughters.

Fern Carness, MPH, RN
Carness Health Management, LLC
PO Box 509
Lake Oswego, OR 97034
(503) 636-7513
(503) 636-5994 fax
ferncarn@teleport.com
www.wise-woman-health.com

My Story

Finally, the nurse brings him to my hospital room, lays him on the bed beside me, and warns, "Don't unwrap him, I'll know if you do." So the minute she goes down the hall I immediately lift the receiving blanket off my new baby and begin to check him out. I am 19 and married for almost two years now. I have a high school diploma and work experience as a coffee-shop waitress. I have less than $50 that is really mine. My mom is not around, and my stepmother is no help. I have no female archetypes to lean on.

I look at him and breathe in his essence. He is beautiful: two eyes, 10 toes, and rosebud lips. His hands are so fascinating. They look exactly like his daddy's hands: every line, every ridge in his fingernails. He takes hold of me and does not let go, creating our first bond. What a miracle. What joy.

Then it hits me. I feel like an imposter. Somebody must know I am not qualified for this job. Yet, he is mine. He came from my body. He drinks milk from my breast, and he clings tightly to me. As the love whelms up first in my chest and then my throat, I also become aware of another emotion. Responsibility. Although I am married to a great man and have family (of sorts), I am profoundly struck with the fact that this child of mine will depend upon me for everything. Others may come and go in his life, but I will always be his mother. The basics – food, clothing, and shelter – are not my concern. It's the other things, the real stuff of life: love, friendship, self-esteem, values, knowledge, spirit, humor, and intellect. It is then that I begin to cry. I am so scared.

How can a 19-year-old high school graduate be responsible for creating the man that he will become? How will I know what to do, what to say, how to give him all that there is to have in life? How can I teach him how to be an authentic person when I hardly know how to be one myself?

So as I cry I also think about what I know that matters in life and what I have of substance to offer him. I realize that I am a pretty smug girl, not exactly self-confident but yet with a sense of worth, an inner confidence. I wonder how I got to feel as if I was somebody. Certainly I did not get this at home. (My dysfunctional childhood could be the topic of an entire book by itself.) As I try to think about who influenced me and how I came to believe in myself, I remember my maternal grandfather, Philly. He loved me so much and always called me Princess. He had a love of reading and a passion for learning that he passed on to me. He used to say, "What you have in your pockets, they will soon take away. But what you have in your head, you keep for ever and a day."

So I begin to plan my son Scott's life chapter by chapter. And I quickly realized that I will need a more solid future if I am going to raise this gifted child. I decide to follow my dream of becoming a nurse. Grandfather Philly had also instilled me with a hunger for education. I remember when I was about three I was incredibly bored during a family reunion at a Chinese restaurant when from nowhere he produces a nurse's kit for me to play with. It only confirmed that I was born to be a nurse.

Back in high school I was a good student but from the wrong side of the tracks if you know what I mean. So my high school guidance counselor suggested that I take typing to get some office skills. He did not offer any college prep information nor was I scheduled to take the SATs. So I had no idea how to go to college. But I was determined to find out.

One sunny morning I plopped Scott, now six months old, into the stroller and set out for the local junior college. I was way too ashamed of my ignorance to ask *anyone* how to get into a college. What were the requirements? How much did it actually cost? Who was eligible? I wouldn't ask because I knew *they* would laugh. Just like the girls had laughed and snickered in high school when I would ask where they bought mohair sweaters. I didn't know which fork to use at dinner with my boyfriend, the doctor's son.

I had grown up knowing that we were lower-class people. Not merely poor but also undereducated and uncultured. I was a voracious reader as a young girl, so I knew enough to notice the difference. What really separated us from them was that they knew stuff we didn't. Like *the theater was not the place you went to watch a movie, most homes have a dictionary, six kids shouldn't share a bedroom, and the police were not always invited to holiday dinners.*

So we walked, Scott and I, around and around that campus for many hours. By a stroke of luck it happened to be "Open Registration Day," which I quickly learned meant that students could sign up for classes that day. As long as I kept the stroller moving, Scott was happy and content. It was almost 10 that night when we got home. Cold, wet diapers, and hungry but amazingly we were enrolled in college. It was official, I was going to learn what *they* knew, and I was going to have a degree to prove it.

It actually took me five years to complete the two-year nursing program. I took classes early in the morning or late at night when my husband could watch our son. I spaced the daytime classes so that my mother-in-law could help. Scott was almost five when he attended my graduation. During those five years he had slept in the stroller at the back of the room in my organic chemistry class; he learned to color in my anatomy and physiology textbooks and had perfect attendance at study lab.

I can now say that I understand how the feelings of inadequacy can come from my upbringing. The sense of being an imposter is strong inside many successful women. My fear was this: What if *they* find out I don't really know it all, what if they see through me and find that scared 19-year-old? And so it continued one degree, certification, or credential after another to prove that I am worthy.

Women who suffer from the imposter syndrome believe that if they obtain more education and pass more tests they will prove that they are knowledgeable with more diplomas and degrees. Interestingly, it is only the woman herself who doubts her expertise. Everyone else thinks she is amazing. At long last I think I am calmer about this and able to trust that I know what I know and you know what you know, and we all know that the only thing that matters is love.

The Imposter Syndrome

Don't let your life's work become your passion.
Rather, take your passion and make it your life's work.

Whenever people hear that I operate my own business, they usually remark how nice it must be to set your own work schedule. I usually reply, yes, I can work any 100 hours a week that I want. Most people have no idea how much goes into owning and running an independent business. People also seem to think that I must be rich since I can set my own salary and write my paychecks. They tend to miss the fact that I must actually obtain the money through selling goods and services and keep the expenses down with shrewd decisions before I can expect to pay myself one cent. That of course is after I pay all the people who help me run the business.

Yet with long hours, nerve-racking responsibility, and sporadic paychecks, I can truly say that I love to work for myself. The thrill of being an entrepreneur allows me to work as hard as I want to make things right. I can honor my own values and work from a place of respect and passion. I can do what I want as long as what I want is what the client will pay for. I make a lousy employee but a great business-woman.

My passion is to use my understanding of health behavior to assist people in taking good care of themselves. Using my gift of gab and a wicked sense of humor I enjoy teaching and coaching women through difficult health-related decisions. My clinical expertise in critical care nursing and my personal experience of breast cancer make me uniquely qualified to serve as a voice for women's health in one capacity or another.

The lessons to be learned in business never cease to amaze me, sometimes with love and humor and sometimes with the sting of irony. I continue to make mistakes, but usually not the same ones twice. I will share a bit of my wisdom in the hope that I can spare you one of my teachable moments.

If you are planning to start a business on your own, you must select your stepping stones carefully and avoid the stumbling blocks I have already tripped over.

Stepping stone: Calculated risk taking is less risky.

Being in business for yourself or in a partnership can be risky business. You have to be able to withstand the financial risk as well as the emotional toll the pride of ownership can exact from your life. The most common reason for a business to fail within the first two years is under capitalization. In plain English, this means you don't start with enough money. Timing is important, wait until you can afford the risk rather than going out in a big but quick splash. Here are a couple of things to keep in mind when considering the risks you will face.

Don't get caught in the money trap.

- Most new businesses can expect to run in the red for at least two years. You will have to be able to pay all of the operating expenses to run your business without depending on revenues for quite a while in the start-up phase. It always takes more money than you think it will. Always.
- You will not be able to take a paycheck until you have cleared all debt. If you start paying yourself before you pay off credit lines, for example, you will be making a big mistake. Credit lines carry interest and paychecks also cost more in taxes. Best

to live off savings and clear debt before cashing your first check.

We must be crazy.

- Owning a business will make you doubt even your most basic instincts. Find a coach who will help you stay clear and on track with your mission.
- If you are in a partnership, I highly recommend that you both see a coach/counselor together. This will help with role delineation and set the framework for resolving differences.
- Join a professional women-owned business group to provide objective feedback, networking, and clarity.

Stepping stone: Stick to the plan, stay on the path.

A business plan helps to describe the business in great detail. More than just your ideas on a cocktail napkin, this is a formal outline of all aspects of the business. A good business plan will help you see if the business makes any sense. Without a plan in writing, you will have trouble getting loans or signing a lease. At the very least you should have the following items in your business plan.

- **How do you want to structure the business?** This is pretty straightforward. Choose your structure, such as sole proprietorship, limited liability company, or corporation, and explain why you chose it. This is where your accountant and lawyer should be talking to each other and to you. It's money well spent.
- **What products or services will you sell?** If you are selling your time as a consultant, you will want to list the various services that you will provide. Pricing will be a challenge for time and intellectual property. If you are selling products, then it may be easier to set prices. Decide if you are to be a low-price leader or selling on the benefit of added value.
- **What are your competitors doing?** Find out who else is doing what you want to do. If no one else is doing it, either you have just invented a better mousetrap or there is no opportuni-

ty and the idea is a trap. It is good to know if your future competitors are doing well and where they are in the lifespan of their business.

- **Who will supply your goods?** Where will you get your raw material for your inventory? Will you be able to buy what you need? Are there any restrictions that you should know about?
- **Who are your customers?** How many are there? Where do they live, how much money do they have? Where do they go for this product or service now? How can you shift them to you?
- **What are the industry trends?** What is happening in the industry, the region, the nation, and the world that will have an impact on your business venture? Woe be it to the Edsel repair man.
- **Do you have a marketing plan?** A marketing plan should contain at least three sections: advertising and branding, public relations and promotion, and customer loyalty/retention plans.

Stepping stone: Surround yourself with wisdom and grace you can trust.

With every business you will need to have others to help you. Whether they are employees, business partners, industry colleagues, or clients, you should be surrounded with people who have attributes that you admire. Early on at my first company I decided that life was too short to do business with unpleasant people, twice. Of course you had to do business with them the first time to know they were difficult. Same thing goes for employees. A lot of people can have the skill set you need to hire, but take the time to look for the candidates who also have grace and wisdom. You'll be glad you did.

Here are a few traits I look for in workmates:

- **Sense of humor:** Nothing makes a workplace more productive than laughing until you wet your pants! I like to feel free to have a good time; I do not believe it reduces productivity at all. This includes customers and clients. Smile, I'll charge you less.

- **Brutal honesty:** I want honest feedback to concepts and ideas. I hate it when I suspect that an employee or colleague is just blowing sunshine to make me feel good. This really fuels my imposter complex. I expect that I can be honest with others and expect the same in return. I have been known to say, "If you don't want to know how I feel about it, don't ask me." Lying to me is the quickest way to be fired.
- **Accountability, not excuses:** I depend heavily upon the folks I work with. I make promises to clients/customers and expect my workmates will help me make it happen. Otherwise we are out of business. Your reputation is fragile and must be beyond reproach. I am dependable and expect the same in return. If you are late, it's disrespectful. If you mess-up, it's OK, just fix it. I hate surprises, talk to me.

Stepping stone: Plan your exit strategy.

Unless you plan to die at your desk and be buried with your day-planner and PDA in hand, you will need an exit strategy. When you start a business, it will help to know how you plan to end the business.

If, for example, you plan to hand the business down in the family for the next 100 years, then you will have a much longer term plan and your interests will not be on ROI in the short run. On the other hand, if you, like me, get bored easily and would like to start the business, get it up and running, and then sell it, you will be concerned about the short-term profitability and the best way to make the business attractive to prospective new owners. Even if you plan to work your business until retirement, the way you run a business has much to do with how you plan to exit. Think about it. It may change your day-to-day structure. Include these items in your exit file.

- Archive a historical set of financial statements to show a trend to prospective new owners.
- Track marketing data including the cost of each program and the results obtained.

- Write down your future plans based on feasibility studies you have conducted. This will attest to the longevity of the business opportunity.
- Keep a list of competitors and colleagues who may have future interest in acquiring your company.
- Exit gracefully and keep your contacts.

In the end, for me, it would have been more of a risk to stay in a job that I hated or worse yet being managed by people I could not trust or respect. So sometimes you have to take a risk to survive. Maybe you are not the imposter you fear, but rather the one who sees clearly one stepping stone at a time and has the courage to be the first one on the path.

On Women and Aging:
Funny You Should Ask . . .

Sandy Queen

Sandy Queen has been entertaining audiences around the world for the past 25 years. Her philosophy? Lighten Up! This is the only life you have! Sandy is the founder and director of Lifeworks, in Columbia, Maryland. Through her wide variety of workshops and keynotes, Sandy's ability to use humor, even for serious topics, has gained her a widespread reputation for helping participants take a look at their lives, attitudes, and feelings, and find places to "lighten up," both personally and professionally.

Sandy Queen
PO Box 2668
Columbia, MD 21044
(410) 992-7665; (800) 401-2202
goodstf@aol.com
www.sandyqueen.com

Sandy Queen

My Story: On Women and Aging:
Funny You Should Ask . . .

The photo shows a little girl and an older woman. I was five. My grandmother, my mother's mother, was already gray-haired, a little knot of hair pulled back on her head; a flowered cotton dress covering generous hips; breasts that had long since lost any sense of "perkiness" – if indeed, that word had even existed to describe what women of my grandmother's generation thought of mainly as Playtex feeders; black orthopedic shoes with stockings rolled down.

How old was she then? The same age I am now: 57. She had her first baby in her teens, and my mother was the sixth of 10 children.

My paternal grandmother was much the same. "Granny Bort" was the only name I ever heard anyone call her. She was short, under 5 feet, always roly-poly with white hair piled on top of her head, topped off by one of her many hats. How old was she when I was five? Early fifties, late forties, I would guess. My dad was the second oldest of eight children, the first being born in my grandmother's late teens.

For the past four years I have participated in the 350-mile AIDS bicycle fund-raiser from Raleigh, North Carolina, to Washington, D.C. This past year, as the 1,600 riders finished our four-day trek and rode into D.C., I was greeted by my cheering section: my three kids and my four grandchildren. My oldest grandchild, Kristi, was 12 at the time. I was 56. As she stood there cheering me in with her sign "Go G.S. Go!" (Grandma Sandy), it occurred to me that her memories of me will be far different from my memories of my grandmothers. And her labels of "old" will be different also.

What part of the hill don't you understand?

Middle age is generally considered to be the age period between 45 and 65. Chronologically, we may be middle-aged, but many of us are refusing to go gently into that age. We refuse to be "over the hill," or "under the hill," but, instead, we prefer to be on top of the hill where we can survey our surroundings and determine our speed and direction for the next part of our journey. We are on uncharted pathways.

My grandmothers never heard of "physical fitness," "wellness," "self-care," "mind/body/spirit health." I'm sure they had no idea what their cholesterol level was, much less their LDLs and HDLs. They probably never even knew what their blood pressure readings were (those were secrets known only to your physician back then).

Fat grams? Carbohydrates? Hey, my mother's mother churned her own butter and baked bread for all three meals, along with frying up all parts of the hog for breakfast.

Best friends? There were too many kids to have time for coffee on the deck (back porch).

My mother's mother had cows to milk, pigs to slop, chickens to feed, bread to bake, and water to draw from the well so she could make her own soap, boil the water, and clean the laundry out in the back yard in three huge cast-iron kettles. At least there were no bathrooms to scour, since the two-holer in the barnyard was the sole "facility," and a metal wash tub on the back porch served Saturday night bath-time rituals.

The evening news? Right. One of the strongest memories of my summers at my grandmother's house was at noon each day, the local funeral home would broadcast over the radio the list of those who had died in the county over the past 24 hours. That was the daily news. Can you imagine a day, a life, without cosmetic commercials, infomercials, CNN, and laundry detergent comparisons?

So who's leading the parade?

Many of us still feel we can do anything . . . if only we knew what that was! This time of our life is made even more difficult as we realize that few of us had any role models. Sure we had Betty Friedan and Gloria Steinem, but then we found out that Gloria had the same insecurities we had, she just hid them better.

The message of the women's movement was not only that as women we **have** potential, but that we must **exercise** all that potential. So we did. We went out and got jobs and put our kids in daycare and helped with the bills – and still came home and did over 90 percent of the housework. Many of us felt a little jaded along the way, a little conflicted, over the traditional roles of women and the new roles we were being asked to assume.

America's Most Wanted

As of the year 2000, 30 percent of all adult women were over the age of 50. We are the fastest growing segment of the population. Everyone is studying us! They all want to know how to get us to use their products (products that, by the way, hadn't even been dreamed of during my grandmothers' lives, and, even if they had been, they wouldn't have been produced because who wanted to market to old women?). They want us! They really really want us!

Yet, many of us still feel the conflicting messages associated with our roles as women and the meanings we have come to attribute to the aging process. After all, once the ovaries close up shop, what's left? Right?

I don't know about you, but I don't want to be labeled based on my birth date or my ovarian capabilities. What is 35 to you? 45? 55? 65? 75? 85? Which age did you label "old"? What images do you hold about this age you have labeled?

As we continue to increase longevity, we continue to move middle age around. Some people predict that soon old age won't start until 80 or 85. In the meantime, we are in the *"My, you don't look 50"* stage. What *does* 50 look like, anyway? Make a list of the characteristics of a "typical" 50-year-old and then go out and see if what you listed is the norm. Bet you will be surprised.

We are "going through a stage" of discovery, or *re*-discovery of our lives. Some of these discoveries are wonderful. Some of them are not. One day you get up and look in the mirror and realize that your body has headed south without you and is never coming north again. The question that many of us ask at this point is, *"Is this It? Is this what I've worked for all these years? Is this all I get?"*

Is it all doom and gloom? Of course not.

- Remember being a teen when you thought everyone was looking at you?
- And then at 21 you hoped *someone* was looking at you.
- At 31 you wondered if *anyone* had ever looked at you.
- At 41 you realized *no one* was looking at you.
- And at 51: *Hey, look at me! What you see is what you get!* And *that* is one of the most freeing times of our lives!

The changing image of aging

We have what it takes to change the image of aging, and we have the numbers. At the turn of the twentieth century, the life expectancy for American women was 51 years. At the turn of this century, 79.

Every 7.5 seconds a baby boomer turns 50. According to the Census Bureau, by 2010 the over-50 population will grow another 30 percent, while the 20-to-49 group will remain about the same. Hey, getting older is a lot more fun when everyone you know is doing it too. Even better if we manage it with style and humor, even though there are some definite truths of aging that, humor or not, we may still have to deal with.

Like . . . if you are over 40, did you wake up one morning wondering where your 20/20 vision went overnight? And remember when you were 20 and wanted to lose a few pounds by the next weekend so you could look good in that little black dress, and you did? Now, you have to plan in advance, months in advance. Seems that our bodies and our fat cells have grown increasingly fond of each other as we age, and they are not easily separated.

Remember when you used to laugh at the ads for the dreaded "age spots" on television? Hmmm? And now . . . where do those little brown spots appear on your body? And what about that bladder? What bladder? Oh yes, your memory has faded too. Now, where was I? (That's why nature will not let us have babies at this age. We would put them down and not remember where!)

And what about realizing that you have become an orphan **and** the matriarch of the family at the same moment? Or that your physician wasn't even born when you graduated from high school? Can you say "orthotics"?

Then, on your fiftieth birthday, at the very moment the anniversary of your birth arrives, so does the invitation to become a card-carrying member of AARP. Hint: Go ahead and pay the 12 bucks or they will continue to send you the mailings. If you don't answer, they will send you life-insurance information because they are sure that if you aren't sending in your membership fee, you must be ready to wave the funeral fans. You can continue paying full price at the motel where you are staying or begin to take advantage of one of the "benefits" of aging.

The "M" word

Notice I haven't mentioned the "M" word to this point. Menopause for some of us made PMS look like a mere bad-hair day. For others, it has been a less taxing time, but for all of us it has been what it is labeled – a "change." Millions of us are entering menopause, and the experts still don't know what to tell us about it. AND, the average 50-year-old woman can expect to live at least one-third of her life after menopause. Remember, Sleeping Beauty was 50 when she finally woke up!

So do you want to spend this big chunk of your life regretting who you are, or do you want to be passionate, adventurous, and sexy. Yes, I said sexy. Many women claim that sex becomes more satisfying than ever after age 50. Compare that to the old image of the dried-up post-menopausal shrews.

The media would lead us to believe that all of us, men and women, need a little help at this age. You've seen the ads: He's on Viagra and she's taking gingko for her memory, to remind him to take his Viagra! The message: Aging is about loss. And so it is, in some form or fashion. But it is also about growing and empowerment and freedom.

In his Seven Stages of Life, Erikson labels this stage as "generativity vs. stagnation" meaning, giving something back to the world vs. sitting still and letting it all pass by. Or as someone noted, it's the difference between living longer or taking longer to die. Your choice.

This is a time of transformations, and not all of them have to do with our physical bodies. It's more than menopause and chair aerobics. It's about becoming strong and learning who we are, remembering that it is our bodies that are wrinkled, not our minds.

Experimentation never stops. Neither does learning that this is the time to stop being responsible *for* and begin to be responsible *to* – our lives, our personal growth, and our continued possibilities for life, love, and adventure.

Therefore, be it resolved:

- Buy some new fluffy towels and get rid of those pieces of sandpaper you dry off with.
- Take a different route – home from work and in your life.
- Practice wisdom (Remember, age doesn't necessarily travel with wisdom; sometimes it comes alone.).

- Choose forgiveness. It takes entirely too much energy to stay angry at someone.
- Go to Nordstrom's and have one of the cosmeticians make you up with amazing colors.
- Take a class; learn something new that has nothing to do with your career.
- Spend a day with a 4-year-old and an 80-year-old;
- Drink lots of water.
- Dance!
- Choose joy.
- Buy a really expensive French-milled bar of luxury soap . . . and use it. Throw away all the little bars you have collected from all the hotels you have stayed in.
- Clean out your underwear drawer. Get rid of the everyday stuff and wear what Loretta LaRoche calls your "party panties" – every day.
- Be nice to yourself, and you'll find yourself being nice to other people as a result.

Now that we're grown up

Want to know what I love about this age?

- No more games. New Rules: the ones we make ourselves.
- Comfortable shoes and clothes (I think I wore my last pair of high heels when I was 45.).
- We can go to a bar or restaurant and sit alone and not pretend that we are waiting for someone to show up. We can be alone and like it.
- We can do what we want, when we want, with whom we want, and not apologize. We can say "I don't know" and not feel guilty or stupid;
- We don't find it necessary to engage in the soap-opera side of life.
- We can stop waiting to look like someone we have never looked like.
- We can start deciding what to be now that we are growing up!

Let's hear it for us!

To paraphrase Helen Reddy: Are we strong? Yes! Are we invincible? Well, I have to admit, there are those days when, after a presentation, a woman will come up to me and say, "You and I are the same age. Isn't that great?" and I want to run screaming into the night. Do I look that **old**? Invincible, no. Are we Woman? Definitely, YES!

This isn't just about those of us who have recently burst into our fifties, but about those we met as we entered this place in our lives, and the rest of you who will join us sooner or later. We need reminders that every age is valuable, and that we need more than the latest Alpha-Hydroxy formula to change the images of middle age. We need to provide examples – **be** the women who make aging something not to be re-worked, retouched, tightened or tucked, but something we look forward to with attitude and grace.

It's about power. Historically, our power has been about our physical looks. Now we need to embrace a new power – a power of mental beauty, emotional beauty. Not that we are ugly. We aren't. These sun spots are a result of wonderful days on the beach. These stretch marks have class. These thigh dimples aren't cellulite, they're *hail   damage*! (Thank you, Rob Sweetgall.) These breasts nursed three babies and saved me from heating bottles in the middle of the night! These legs— "unsightly spider veins" and all—have carried me on four 350-mile bike rides, with all the training miles leading up to them and seven marathons! These brown eyes – the same ones that a farm boy told me at 16 reminded him of his Jersey calf (ah, romance!) are the same brown eyes – bifocaled but still beautiful. This body is a powerhouse of beauty and strength! How about yours?

I love it that most of us are a great, noisy, fun-loving, self-accepting bunch of middle-aged women. Over the next few years we will create a whole new image of age.

C'mon! You are as young as you are ever going to be at this moment. Live it up! Celebrate!

Rest in peace, my grandmothers. I carry the gift of your strength.

Reinvent Yourself:
Reflect, Review, Re-do, RENEW

Carol Ebert, RN, BSN, MA, CHES

Carol Ebert, nurse and education specialist, has an extensive and varied professional career in health care, corporate wellness, and community health. A pioneer in the wellness movement, she has successfully integrated these concepts into the current health care system – not an easy task. Her persistent nature keeps the flame alive despite cutbacks, downsizing, mergers, and the rapid change of business today. Carol's gift of creativity allows her to develop award-winning programs as well as to shift gears quickly to adapt to whatever change is coming. She enjoys the challenge of today's unsettled workplace.

A master teacher, an expert in lifestyle management, and an unstoppable creative force for organizational change, Carol is sought after as a speaker and trainer for wellness, stress management, self-care, creativity, and coaching. She is a high-energy, action-oriented speaker with a contagious zest for life. Her message is relevant and compelling, her style personable, her approach sincere. Humor and fun are on her agenda, and Carol's passion and enthusiasm for education and wellness is infectious.

Carol Ebert RN, BSN, MA, CHES
Personal Coach and Wellness Specialist
Ebert and Associates
Route 1, Box 40
Dakota, MN 55925
(507) 643-6436
carol@ebertandassociates.com
www.ebertandassociates.com

My Story

I am a nurse. A fortuitous career choice for me with a penchant for change and a need to reinvent myself on a regular basis. My first revelation: I am not a nurse in the traditional sense – patient care expert. I am a nurse in the global sense, caring about total health – mind, body, and spirit. Luckily, my nursing path led me to wellness, my true passion, where I spent the majority of my career. Even within my passion, however, I still found a need to reinvent myself regularly.

Why this desire to change? Born with a creative brain, I am often plagued with frustration when working in a structured and predictable environment. I can do it if I have to, thanks to an authoritarian upbringing and being educated in a rule-oriented school system. But it is not my true nature. I discovered this only after I reached adulthood when I finally was able to fully express who I was. Breaking out of that structured mold was a must.

And I did. Listening to my inner voice saying "do something different with your life," I became a Navy nurse during the Vietnam era. A road not often taken, it was different, eye-opening, shocking, brutal, fun, maturing, romantic, and the best first step in my evolution. I reinvented myself from a standard cookie-cutter fledgling nurse to a military officer. My pattern was set. There was no turning back. My inner wisdom had set the wheels in motion for an unpredictable nursing career filled with variety, interest, and challenges.

Civilian life brought me back to "sameness" once more. Not content caring for the sick, I embarked on school nursing, which was ripe territory for entering the world of health education, an emerging passion for me. A wise mentor encouraged me to pursue an advanced degree in health education. I began to teach, and loved it. Soaring now, I was starting to emerge from the restrictive box I had built around myself.

More challenges ahead – tackling a college health directorship. This great experience seemed right for me, despite cautionary words from colleagues that I couldn't handle it. They were wrong. I was successful, but stayed with it too long.

Once again, another opportunity opened. The old turf of the health care system was calling me back with all the structure I had left behind. Not willing to cower in the face of a challenge, and armed with my expertise in wellness, I entered the old familiar world of "medical model" thinking. With high expectations of bringing the wellness message forward in this world of "fixing" not preventing, and with my usual positive and persistent nature, I succeeded.

Then something changed. I felt it in my soul. My inner voice was shouting again to make a change. And this was the big one. The organization had changed. I was being swallowed again by rules. I'd lost my joy of work. My inner voice was screaming – move on! But I didn't listen, I thought I could last. Just a few more years and you can retire. Hold on you can do it.

As stress-pain and mental anguish took its toll, the process of reinventing myself began once more. Life's internship was over. I had done enough, experienced enough, matured enough, proven myself enough, been successful enough. The real test was to survive and flourish on my own, free of the hypnotic tug of financial security and benefits. My "can do" attitude took on the challenge.

Today, my creative side is alive and well. Free from constraints, I am continually reshaping and designing my own grand plan for my life's work. I haven't been alone in this process. Many wise people along the way have been there for me. I've learned many lessons and discovered many simple strategies that have brought me joy. I therefore share real words of wisdom from other women as well as personal success tools for anyone wishing to reflect, review, re-do, and renew. This is about risk taking, using a reasonable approach. Not all these tools work for everyone, but they all have worked for me. Try a few and see what happens. You might be surprised. Let your journey begin.

Reinvent Yourself: Reflect, Review, Re-do, RENEW

Re-view your situation

Awareness is an important first step in the change process. Consider a quick personal assessment of your situation, be honest with yourself, and be open to what you discover.
- What are you doing with your life?
- What is your body, mind, and spirit telling you about what you are doing?

Live an extraordinary life – one grounded in personal truth, sourced from Spirit, and danced with joy.

– *Tracy Carreon,* MA, Speaker and Life Coach

Re-spond to body signals

A wake-up call for change often manifests itself as pain resulting from stress. Headaches, neck and shoulder pain, back aches, indigestion, insomnia, and other ails.
- What physical signs are you experiencing that might indicate stress overload and imbalance?
- What other signs of imbalance are you aware of emotionally, intellectually, spiritually, socially, and occupationally?

Reinventing ourselves is about creating balance in our lives. We want to be able to pet our dogs and cats while we are on the telephone! That is the life I designed for myself.

– *Teri Sullivan,* President, Sulli & Associates, Inc.

Re-spect your inner voice

Our internal voice – the voice of our truth – may be giving us messages and needs to be heard. Access this important information by taking time to slow down, quiet your mind, get comfortable with stillness, and find a way to meditate that is right for you. Turn off the world's input for awhile and just "be."

- How can you practice quieting your mind? Consider meditation, prayer, gentle movement, walking in solitude.
- What happens when you quiet your mind? What messages do you receive?

Listen more than talk. Pay attention to the
messages that come to you.

– Marge Johnson

Re-solve to move forward

Being in your comfort zone is just that – comfortable. But it may not be the best place for you. Get un-comfortable for a while. Practicing new behaviors feels awkward at first, but through repetition it gets easier.
- What action steps will you take to move forward?
- How will you deal with the discomfort that might arise?

I have reinvented myself several times and am always
'at risk' of leaving the more comfortable environment
of 'what I knew to be true.' I then try to apply those
same principles to something else.

– Christine Valenti, Off-Campus Coordinator,
Graduate Program for Teachers, Viterbo University

Re-kindle your passion

Operating from your true passion means getting lost in the energy it provides. You find yourself enjoying what you are doing so much that time doesn't matter and you feel alive, productive, and energized. It's no longer work. It's fun.
- When have you felt the most alive?
- How much time do you currently devote to this?

Calm seas don't make good sailors.

– Kay Wais, PMP, Successful Projects, LLC

Re-move obstacles

What blocks you from realizing your dreams? Is it a true obstacle or a false belief about yourself? Consider breaking it down into small components and chipping away, a bit at a time. You can't move a large boulder, but you can chisel off small rocks, until it's manageable enough to push aside.

- What is one roadblock standing in the way of your progress?
- How can you break it down into small action steps to make it more manageable?

I've always likened myself to a free bird . . . soaring and racing its way through the sky, just as in life. And then without warning to save my life, one of my wings was taken away. What I found out about myself is that I can fly with one wing.

– Marsha Blank, written after a diagnosis of breast cancer, Founder of Women Who Care breast cancer support group

Re-place old behaviors

Hanging on to old behaviors that once were useful but now are not may prevent you from moving forward. Example: not speaking up when you have the opportunity because you think what you have to say is not important, not eloquent, not good enough. A wise woman said to me, "If not now, when are you finally going to express who you really are? What are you waiting for?"

- What is one old behavior you cling to that isn't getting you what you want?
- What is the worst thing that could happen if you changed this behavior?
- What are you willing to do to change this behavior?

What you think about, you bring about!

– Jill A. Blokhuis, MS, Associate Director of Development, Gundersen Lutheran Medical Foundation, Community Volunteer

Re-frain from negativity

At any given time you have two choices – to be negative or to be positive. Do you choose to laugh, have fun, see the bright side of every-thing - or not? A positive "can do" attitude will serve you well as you journey through the reinventing process.

- Describe a situation in which you focused on the negative.
- Describe the same situation using a positive approach. How are they different for you?

I am reminded not to waste my time on things I don't want in my life. Life is too short. Refocus on what you want to happen in your life and go forward in that direction.

– Clare Sente, MS, RD, "truth seeker"
Corporate Account Executive, GCG Financial, Inc.,

Re-spond differently

Change can be difficult, because it is often about the unknown. Without change, nothing new, interesting, better, and more fulfilling occurs.

- If you were to make a change, what would it look like?
- How willing are you to let go of a predictable future and see where it leads you?

"I believe that the Universe has some great plans for all of us, and by controlling what we think should/could happen, it is limiting us from what we don't realize could be possible."

– Pamela Gavrill, RN, HNC, Certified Holistic Nurse,
The Healing Place, Presenter, Workshop Coordinator,
Wisdom Way Productions

Re-frame your thinking

Ever notice when you change the color of a picture frame, differ-ent parts of the picture stand out more vibrantly than before? Are you willing to reframe your vision to find out what new looks and directions emerge?

- Consider sitting quietly with your eyes closed and picturing what your life looks like now. Fill in all the details and the colors.
- Now picture a life filled with complete happiness and joy. How is it the same? How is it different?

All things are made new if we open ourselves to that which is being created in us, around us and in each moment of our lives. We are here to say YES to life.

– *Katherine Murphy,* Health and Wellness
Manager, Mindful Coach

Re-state your assets

How often do you focus on your talents, skills, abilities, deeds, successes? Or do you tell yourself, "I did this wrong – I made a mistake – I forgot to do this – I should have known better." Getting caught up in this self-talk reduces positive energy and your ability to move forward.

- Consider making a list of all the good things about you.
- How might this list be useful for you?

What I do when I get off the path, and am struggling to get back on, is slow down, think of how I am blessed with so many good things, pray, and then take time to listen. If I 'really' listen, the answer and direction is usually there.

– *Carol Berra,* RN

Re-late your true vision

Living your true vision brings joy and fulfillment. Even if you are not living it fully at present, speak about it. Send the message out into the universe, and you will have made a commitment to realize that dream.

- What is your dream?
- What are you telling others about your dream?

*When you feel powerless, toss your thoughts and
questions out to the Universe, and let yourself be
guided by the universal life energy force.*

– *Diane L. H. Peeso,* woman, friend, nurse, massage
therapist, owner Tranquility Massage Therapy and Bodywork

Re-assess your career

Unfulfilling work affects your attitude and a bad attitude is hard
to turn off. It can spill over into other important areas of your life and
affect quality time with family and friends.
- How does your work fulfill you?
- How does your work tie to your passion and joy?

*As I have grown older, wiser, and more enriched in life,
I know how important it is to not worry about the little things
and experience everything. Try everything on for size, you
will find the passions that fulfill your life.*

– *Jean Marie Krause,* Mentor/coach,
Quality Improvement Consultant

Re-store your energy

Most people are exhausted most of the time, which is a perfect
excuse for not being active. The less active you are, the more tired you
get. Moving forward on a new path takes energy. Adding exercise to
your day provides that energy boost by reducing stress, helping you
sleep better, and lightening your load by burning off excess calories
and fat.
- How much regular activity do you have in your life?
- How can you start the process of being active every day?

*The thing I do consistently when I'm stuck or troubled is
breathe deeply and move in some creative way. When I do this,
I take myself into a new place and it reaffirms my abilities
and power. This also connects me with my innate knowing;
once there I regain my balance and momentum.*

– *Suzanne Kilkus,* MA, Entrepeneur,
Co-owner Heartspace Coaching

Re-fuel your body

Stamina is required for you to reach your goals. Keeping your body nourished provides even more energy as you grow in other healthy ways. Good food, in the right amounts at the right times, and drinking lots of water for brain power are some refueling tips.
- What is your awareness of the effect of what you eat on your body and mind?
- What are you willing to do to provide your body with what it requires for peak performance?

The type and amount of food I eat directly affects
my energy level, ability to think clearly, and my mood.
I am in charge of how 'sharp' I am at any given time.

– Carol Ebert

Re-new your spirit

Just like your physical body, your spirit needs tending as well. Adding fun, laughter, and play into your day opens you to the renewal that lies ahead.
- What strategies do you use to nourish your spirit?
- How much time do you spend each week on these strategies?

We all need to laugh more often. We take
ourselves too serious, way too serious.

– Theresa J. Erickson, Hattiesburg Clinic

Re-claim relationships

Reinventing yourself is less scary when you gather the support and wisdom from others who have done this work before you. Pick their brains. The hardest part is doing the asking.
- Who are people you know who have reinvented themselves?
- When can you schedule time on your calendar to connect with them?

Wise Women Speak

Use the phone more! It's a sure way to stay connected.

– Ruby Petersen Unger, Educational filmmaker,
Unger Productions

Re-ward yourself

Instead of relying on others to reward you, consider what you can do for yourself to celebrate progress. You are responsible for your own joy.
- What are healthy pleasures for you?
- How can you make these healthy pleasures become rewards for you?

I stick an encouraging phrase on my bathroom mirror and front door. Any phrase for any particular day – 'You are going to enjoy this day.' 'You are going to brighten someone else's day today.'— whatever comes to mind.

– Shirlene Thomas, woman on the move

Re-group regularly

The present moment is all we have. It's where to focus our energy to do the most good. Practicing "present moment thinking" on a regular basis lightens your load and reduces your stress, making the daily footwork toward your goals easier.
- What do you find your mind focusing on most of the time – past, present or future?
- What is one thing you can do to bring your mind back to the present moment?

I have discovered the importance of really slowing down and enjoying the present moment. I call it my 'just be' time. It has added so much to my life as I have learned to slow down and appreciate what is right before my eyes.

– Stephanie Mitchell, MS, CHES, Life Coach,
White Belt NIA Instructor, Health Promotion Manager,
Arlington County Government

Re-tain your true self

You are unique and no one is like you. When you are being real and honest with yourself, everything becomes clear and you know what you are here for.

- How would life be if you were totally honest with yourself?
- What are you willing to do to become more honest with yourself?

> *'The flowers of tomorrow are in the seeds of today.'*
> *When I think of these words, I am reminded that*
> *personal growth takes time, nourishment, and care*
> *from the beginning in order to continue to reach*
> *our goal of full-flowering development as*
> *an individual.*

> *– Vlasta Karol Blaha*, Educator, Naturalist,
> School Library Media Director

And now you're on your way. Enjoy the process of reinvention!